PEBBLES
of
PERCEPTION

How A Few
Good Choices Make
All The Difference

PEBBLES
of
PERCEPTION

How A Few
Good Choices Make
All The Difference

Laurence Endersen

ISBN-10: 1502458578
ISBN-13: 978-1502458575
Published by Laurence Endersen.
First published 2014 (print and electronic)
Laurence Endersen © 2014

Illustration and Production Design by Philip Barrett
www.blackshapes.com

Permissions
Extract from *The Invitation* By Oriah Mountain Dreamer from her book, THE INVITATION © 1999. Published by HarperONE. All rights reserved. Presented with permission of the author.
www.oriah.org

To my friends, especially my best friend Kathy.

To Sarah, Laurence and Louise, who I hope will read this someday.

Contents

Acknowledgements

I would like to thank the following people for their direct help with proofreading, their thoughtful suggestions and most of all their encouragement.

Alan Burke, Stan Carey, Alan Copps, Aidan Corcoran, Anne Marie Curtin, Kathy Endersen, Michelle Endersen (who kindly endured and enriched multiple drafts), John Finnegan, Leo Foley, Philip Frankling, John Forde, John Jeffery, Angela Kinnen, John Leahy, Paul McCarthy, Joe Molloy, Deirdre Morgan, Barry Murray, John O'Brien, Patrick O'Brien, David O'Flynn, Valerie O'Flynn, Ronan O'Houlihan, Brian O'Kane, Brian O'Kelly, Angela O'Reilly, Niall O'Sullivan, Shane Parrish, Paul Reidy, Adrian Toner, and Ian Young

I appreciate each of you taking the interest and the time.

I want to particularly acknowledge Brian O'Kelly for showing me what's important, and Alan Burke, who provided me with the opportunity to pursue what I enjoy doing for a living.

Over the years I have also learned vicariously through the writings of others. You may recognise influences from some great minds. These are referenced where appropriate. Any omissions are not intentional. We are subliminally influenced more than we recognise. Mistakes are mine alone.

Introduction

Too soon old, too late wise.

What if this didn't need to be the case?

In September 2007 I turned 40. One of my birthday gifts was a book written by Charlie Munger called *Poor Charlie's Almanack*. For those of you who don't know Charlie Munger, he is best known as the straight-talking business partner of Warren Buffett. Together Charlie and Warren built one of the most successful investment companies in the world. They did it from scratch and they did it in a principled manner.

The Almanack lay untouched on my bookcase for three years before I finally took the time to read it. Studying it revealed the reflections of a man who has thought deeply about how the world works. I was so taken with the Almanack that I wrote to Charlie on my 43rd birthday to thank him for sharing his wisdom. I also committed to write a book myself before I reached 50. So here I am with a personal take on life as inspired by someone whose approach instantly resonated with me, you know the way something simply hits you between the eyes.

There were two big ideas that I took from Charlie's work. The first is the value of understanding the main principles of a wide range of disciplines. These include law, science, maths, statistics, politics, economics, psychology, psychiatry and so on. Scientific principles and human behaviour combine in numerous ways. You don't need to be an expert, but there is immense value in understanding the cornerstones. In all disciplines a few big ideas carry most of the freight. The important thing is not to ignore any of the main disciplines, because life is one big bundle of interconnectedness. Your chances of understanding what's really going on are much better if you look at the world through a multidisciplinary lens. Decisions are wiser when we appreciate how the larger cogs turn.

The second big idea I took from Charlie's work, and the inspiration for this book, is the importance of good choices. Just a few good choices can make all the difference.

Some of the material for this book came from the responses to the following question which I have been posing to anyone who will listen: "Imagine you are dying and have no material wealth. You are allowed to pass on one or two pieces of thoughtful and useful advice to your young adult children. This is the only inheritance you can leave behind – thoughtful advice that they will understand and apply in their lives. What would that advice be?" The range of responses I received was fascinating. It was also quite a personal insight into the respondents. Their advice showed what they truly valued, what really matters. What would your advice be?

They say that you can't put a wise head on young shoulders. But can we not be a little more wise, a little earlier? This is our quest: to see if we can be smarter, earlier. Avoid the "too soon old, too late wise" camp and sign up for the "wiser earlier" expedition.

The "lessons from life" theme has been covered by numerous authors. So what makes this book any different? I hope you will find that it is both reflective and practical – covering thinking and doing. This is a short book: short on words but hopefully long on insight.

The structure of this book is built around three core themes:

Curiosity;

Character; and

Choice.

Curiosity and character provide the foundation for good choices. Our call to action is to be curious, build character and make better choices. With fuel in our tank and tread on our tyres the journey is all ours.

PART I
CURIOSITY
(The Why)

Curiosity: *Eagerness to know or find out.*
Inquisitiveness. Interest. A thirst for knowledge.

Curiosity is the engine of civilisation.
All discovery begins with a question.

What's your question?

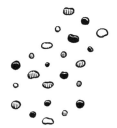

Chapter One:
Is There a Better Question?

I keep six honest serving-men
(They taught me all I knew);
Their names are What and Why and When
And How and Where and Who
                              - Rudyard Kipling

Staying Curious

Why did it take us so long to start putting wheels on suitcases?

If our goal is to become wiser earlier, we are well served by understanding the power of questions. We came into this world with abundant curiosity. As children we were inherently curious, joyfully wondering while wandering. Exploration preceded explanation. Over time many things conspired to dampen our curiosity. Fear of failure is a big inhibitor. So is fear of looking stupid when our ego, or our pay cheque, is tied up in not looking stupid. Young children don't have this fear because their ego has not yet consumed them.

The challenge for us all is to stay curious. Whoever coined the phrase "Curiosity killed the cat" did society a great disservice. In fact, it may also be a misinterpretation of the original phrase "Care killed the cat" – *care* in that context signifying *worry*. I was chatting about this recently with a friend who said that his mum used to retort, "Curiosity killed the cat, *but information brought him back.*" My advice: forget about the cat and stay curious. Adopt the motto ABC: Always Be Curious.

Good Questions Trump Smart Answers

We can be too quick to blurt out what we believe are the correct answers, when more value can be gained by searching for a better question. A questioning mentality is far more effective than a knowing mentality. Once we have declared an answer, our biases towards commitment and consistency cause us to defend our answer, wasting energy that would be better applied to exploring alternatives. A thoughtful colleague of mine sometimes responds to a question with: "I think a more useful question you might want to ask me is...". His thought process shows an all too rare appreciation of why we need care in crafting our questions.

Consider the following puzzle. You are organising a soccer tournament with 32 teams. It is a knock-out format with one winner. How many matches need to be played to determine a winner? You can work through the maths. Alternatively you can consider a different question, such as how many teams need to lose to produce one winner. This will get you to the answer more quickly and it will work instantly for larger and more awkward numbers of teams.

Entrepreneurs and innovators can relate to Kipling's honest serving-men. While good managers ask *how* questions, innovators also ask *why, why not* and *what if* questions. Innovators can combine healthy scepticism with a lack of cynicism. They proceed with a mind that is open to possibility.

First and Second-Level Thinking

I was introduced to this topic through the writings of investor Howard Marks. First-level thinking focuses on the most visible and immediately obvious answer. It is clear to everyone. By contrast second-level thinking considers what else might be going on. This is not immediately obvious. Continually asking ourselves *why* allows us to go beyond first-level thinking. Let's say that you have recently done exceptionally well for yourself. Decisions are going your way and everything is going swimmingly in both your interpersonal and financial affairs. First-level thinking might lead you to conclude that you are smart and in control. Second-level thinking suggests that there may be a large element of luck involved and that you need to keep your ego in check. The illusion of control is pervasive among first-level thinkers.

Richard Feynman, whom we will meet in the next chapter, liked to point out the difference between knowing what something is called and knowing what it is – that is, the difference between knowing the name of something and really knowing something. If I can point to an animal and identify it as a honey badger and I can also tell you what it is called in ten other languages, it doesn't mean that I know anything useful about the honey badger. All it tells you is what humans in different cultures label it. If we really want to know the honey badger, we need to observe it closely and to reflect on what we see.

Questions in Group Settings

Whenever you find yourself in a group forum that is tackling some topic, ask a question! You will be waking up the group to a possibility that is waiting to be explored. Are we asking the right questions here? Are we missing any potentially more useful questions? Or who might help us frame the right questions?

We should always be prepared to re-frame the problem that is being explored. If we head off in the wrong direction, speeding up isn't going to help us no matter how energetic and enthusiastic we are.

If we search for better questions, ultimately to lead to a better answer, we should be prepared to act on that answer even if it contradicts our view of the world, in fact *especially* if it contradicts our world view. This is hard for most of us, but it is a hallmark of emotional maturity.

Better Conversations

When we ask open questions the quality of our conversation improves. Edward de Bono wrote a book called *How to be Interesting* which might be summarised in two words: Be interested. Ask questions and let your tone be gentle and inquisitive.

Good *if* questions stimulate rich debate. For example, what would you do *if* you were not afraid? *If* you could be known for one thing, what would you like that to be?

Why are we not enjoying life to the full? *What* if we did more of what we enjoy and less of what we find dreary or soul-destroying? *How* do we go about changing our priorities? This *why, what-if* and *how* sequence can be the key to possibility, which, let's be honest, is far more interesting than complaining about the status quo.

Stay curious. Improve the quality of questions before getting to work on answers. Use more questions to see beyond the obvious answers. Improve group dynamics by ensuring there is enough attention given to asking the right questions. Be interested.

Chapter Two:
Lifelong Learning

By three methods we may learn wisdom:
First, by reflection, which is noblest;
second, by imitation, which is easiest; and
third, by experience, which is the bitterest.
— Confucius

When we are captain of our own ship, life can be a wonderful continuous voyage of discovery. Yet we frequently pigeonhole our learning and discovery into limiting discrete blocks. There are the childhood years, filled with exploration and getting to know the world around us at a sensory level. The early school years follow, during which we are introduced to reading and writing. Middle school years bring a range of core subjects and some people will finish up the formal part of their education with university-level learning. To this we add work experience, reach a level of competence, and sort of coast our way through life from there. In short, we settle. At a certain level of competence we can navigate life pretty well, so the incentive to keep learning is not always obvious to us. Excessive ego is also a discovery dampener.

When assessing our competence in any particular discipline, we can place our level of ability somewhere along a continuum moving from ignorance, to conversational competence, to operational competence, then towards proficiency, and finally all the way to mastery. For most of us, if we get to operational competence in our main career area we are happy enough. We can get by and we don't have to expend too much energy continuously learning. We become what I call flat-line learners. For the flat-line learner the learning curve might look something like this:

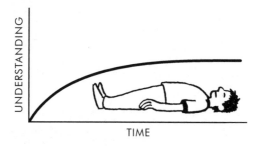

By contrast, should we decide to become lifelong learners, our learning curve will look more like this.

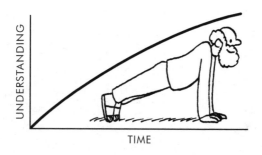

This raises the question: Why doesn't everyone become a lifelong learner? It may boil down to choices and priorities. It is easy to be drawn towards passive entertainment, which requires less from us, over more energetic, active understanding. Inconvenience might be an alibi: "I don't have time for continuous learning as I am too busy with real life". But that excuse doesn't withstand close scrutiny, as experiences (coupled with reflection) can be the richest of all sources of investigation and discovery.

Why not make a conscious decision to learn something new every day? No matter how small the daily learning, it is significant when aggregated over a lifetime. Resolving early in life to have a continuous learning mindset is not only more interesting than the passive alternative, it is also remarkably powerful. Choosing lifelong learning is one of the few good choices that can make a big difference in our lives, giving us an enormous advantage when practised over a long period of time.

Having resolved to be lifelong learners we have two main avenues: directly through our own experiences, and indirectly through learning from the experiences of others. While both avenues have their place, there is no substitute for direct learning through experience – which we enhance through reflection. The process of thoughtful reflection makes our experiences more concrete, and helps with future recall and understanding. Reflecting about what we learned, how we felt, how we and others behaved, and what interests were at play, hardwires the learning in our brain and gives us a depth of context and relevance that would otherwise be absent.

Unfortunately there isn't enough time to learn everything through direct experience. Indeed, this is neither practical nor always desirable, especially when it comes to mistakes. Far better to learn from the mistakes of others, if we can. Whether it is through reading, listening, or watching others in action, there are concrete ways to make our indirect learning more effective.

Reading is the fountain of indirect learning. We can find ample time for reading if we are sufficiently motivated to learn. We can create more opportunities to read by watching less TV, taking public transport instead of driving, and always having reading material close to hand (much easier now with the advent of electronic readers).

Yet how many times have you read a good book and when asked what the most interesting parts were, you could only remember one or two things from the entire book! To avoid this fate we could do worse than start out by reading Mortimer Adler's *How to Read a Book*. I must confess that I read it only recently. Had I read it sooner I am sure I would have a better recollection of much of my previous reading. Many read for entertainment. Some read for information. Too few read for understanding. Adler's book is concerned with reading to understand. Being widely read is not the same as being well read. The more effort and skill we put into reading, the greater our understanding. Adler introduces four levels of reading skill, each building on the former. The first is elementary reading. This is what we learn in school. On an elementary reading we can recall what a book *says*. Next comes inspectional reading from which we can deduce what the book *is about*. We get the gist of it and the general context. Beyond this level we can step up to analytical reading, from which we can explain what the book *means*. Analytical reading is at the root of understanding. We are underlining and marking up as we go along, circling key words, writing in the margins and making various notes. It is a deliberate and focused form of reading. Beyond analytical reading we can progress to the highest and most demanding form, which Adler calls syntopical reading. Here we are evaluating how the book compares with other books on the same topic.

How do we test whether we really understand something? A powerful yet deceptively elegant technique was devised by the late American physicist Richard Feynman.

Step 1. Choose the topic or concept that you are trying to understand. Take a blank piece of paper and write the name of the topic at the top.

Step 2. Assume you're teaching the topic to someone else. Write out a clear explanation of the topic, as if you were trying to teach it. A great way to learn is to teach. You identify gaps in your knowledge very quickly when trying to explain something to someone else in simple terms.

Step 3. If you get bogged down, go back to the source materials. Keep going back until you can explain the concept in its most basic form.

Step 4. Go back and simplify your language. The goal is to use your own words, not the words of the source material. Overly elaborate language is often a sure sign that you don't fully understand the concept. Use simple language and build on that with a clear analogy. An example that springs to mind is Warren Buffet's explanation of compound interest (i.e., interest earned on interest), when he likened it to a snowball that gathers snow as it rolls down a hill.

Choose lifelong learning over flat-line learning. Savour experiences as opportunities to learn. Reflect on your experiences. Read regularly. Learn how to read for understanding. Know how to test whether you really understand something by demonstrating that you could teach it in simple terms with a clear analogy.

The best way to approach learning is with childlike curiosity and a questioning mindset.

Chapter Three:
Listening

*One of the most beautiful qualities of
true friendship is to understand and to be
understood.*

- Seneca

When it comes to describing much of what currently passes for personal communication, the analogy of the crocodile is an apt one: all mouth and no ears.

You may recall your parents telling you that you have two ears and one mouth for a reason. Yet many of us have never really learned to listen. As a distinctly social species this is quite a tragedy. Communication is arguably the most important life skill of all. The quality of human relations is in large part determined by the quality of communication. There are talkers and there are listeners, but we don't learn much, if anything, while we are talking.

Communication comprises both transmitting and receiving. The main focus of this chapter is on receiving. We receive messages through hearing, seeing, feeling and perceiving. But information doesn't enter the brain directly. It passes through our eyes, ears and other sense organs before being processed by our brain. We receive information through the "lenses" we are wearing. We are going to consider two types of communication lens: what I call the *lecturing lens* and the *learning lens*. Each of us has a default tendency towards one or the other. Which is your default mode?

First let's meet the lens distorters.

The lens distorters

The lens distorters frustrate clear communication, like mist on a windscreen. Here are some of the most common distorters.

The limits of language. There are a few distorters at work here. To begin with, verbal communication represents just a small part of overall communication. When we speak to each other we are essentially blowing air at each other – albeit in a highly sophisticated fashion. Phone calls are far less effective than face-to-face encounters. Secondly, we are not always able to find the right words. Words are often not specific enough. We have a word for friend and a word for enemy. What about someone in between? An acquaintance perhaps? What about a work colleague that you respect and trust but would not want to socialise with? Even black and white are not black and white. I recently met the head of an international thread manufacturer that produced over 200 different shades of "white" thread!

Different histories and cultures. Your lens and my lens will have been shaped by our individual histories and conditioning. Words, gestures or tones that may seem humorous and harmless to me could seem offensive to you.

Different contexts. In addition to unique histories, everyone has a different current context and emotional state. We look at the importance of recognising context dependency in more detail in Chapter Five.

Irrational expectation of rationality. When we communicate we expect that logic is what drives other people's behaviour. The reality is that much more is at play and you will waste a lot of time in this world trying to move people through brute logic.

What is your default lens?

Are you more likely to be a talker or a listener? Animated or observant? Focused on yourself or on the other person? I characterise those of us who are more likely to be talkers as wearing the *lecturing lens*. Gaps in conversation are simply periods during which we gather our thoughts to continue our lecture – me and my story. Others are better listeners and tend to communicate through a *learning lens*. I suspect that good listeners are in the minority, which makes defaulting to the *learning lens* all the more effective. There can be no real understanding without listening. We feel honoured when others take a genuine interest in understanding our position. When people understand us we are psychologically validated. Our opinion matters. We matter.

What follows are some suggestions for better communication with others.

Make the learning lens your default setting. Approach every conversation with an open mind. OK, I have a view and I believe it to be the correct one, *but*, what might I be missing here? What if the other person has some insight that can illuminate my own? What if I am wrong? We listen intently not just with our ears, but with our eyes and our senses. We are paying attention, striving to perceive what is really going on in the other person's mind. And they know and appreciate it. The whole conversation is a journey of discovery not a battle of wits.

Make them a star. Try to bring out the best in other people. This is not false flattery, but helping people get their views properly heard and understood. Do not seek to show off how smart you are.

Be courteous. There is no need for rudeness. Respect the right of someone to have a different opinion from yours. Leave *unconstructive* criticism at the door. There is no good in it. It merely creates resentment and distorts the other person's lens, often for a long time. If you call a person an idiot, both you, and the person you insulted, have changed. No apology can take back the words. Avoid criticising people in print or in front of others.

Double check your gut feelings. For example, first impressions can trigger subconscious negative emotions. The person resembles someone you had a problem with, and you suddenly dislike them. Abraham Lincoln understood this risk. When he met someone he didn't like, he resolved to get to know them better.

Find your words. Once you have demonstrated a full understanding of the other person's view, think carefully about what you want to say and then don't say it! Try instead to figure out what the other person is likely to hear. In other words, try to make some allowance for the distortions in their lens. Your opinion on something is more credible when you can also clearly articulate the contrary view. Good communicators are thoughtful in how they choose and arrange their words.

Words are never enough. Your tone and demeanour should be consistent with, and supportive of, the whole message.

Choose quality over quantity. Don't always feel there is a need to fill every moment with communication.

Know when to give or accept an apology. A genuine apology, offered sincerely and accepted, is one the most emotionally mature human interactions.

Don't be a crocodile, all mouth and no ears. Choose a learning lens over a lecturing lens. Be aware of the differences between your lenses and those of others. To truly listen to others is a gift to them. Give it with courtesy and humility. The payback is real understanding.

Chapter Four:
Incentives

*The rabbit runs faster than the fox, because
the rabbit is running for his life while the fox
is only running for his dinner.*
　　　　　　　　　　　　- Richard Dawkins

During my early thirties I went to a lot of
weddings. Most of the best man speeches are
long since forgotten, except for one where the
best man said: "At events like these it is customary to
thank the hotel staff. But I believe that they get paid
to do a job". And he moved on to his next topic. I am
not sure what was worse, the silence in the room, or
the fact that I was the only one laughing. For some
reason it struck a chord with me, even if it was slightly
off key.

Incentives Matter

If we are looking to satisfy our curiosity, we need to
be alive to the impact of incentives. Incentives matter
a *lot*. They are what drive behaviour, and we underestimate their power at our peril. We can only see
a situation with true clarity when we take the time

to carefully consider the interests at hand. And we understand it even better when we consider how the situation might be different if the underlying interests were different.

We don't need to look very hard to see incentives in operation. We work and get paid, we study, we train, we take time preparing a nice meal, all with a payoff in sight. Most of us understand the potential conflict of paying our builders by the hour rather than for the job. In these situations the main incentives at play are obvious. Before I read a newspaper article I usually look at the background of the author, if disclosed, not just to weigh credibility, but also to consider whether any particular incentives might be behind the line of reporting.

The Distorting Power of Incentives (or the "Pointed Carrot")

If we want a laboratory for understanding the distorting power of incentives, the world of investment banking is a good place to start. Paying people a substantial share of profits without having to bear losses is highly likely to result in excessive risk-taking. The "eat what you kill" culture is bound to compromise teamwork. In this respect the system is doing all its participants a disservice. I guess if I were part of such a system I would be as vulnerable as the next guy. Notwithstanding this, I like to think of myself as a reasonable person, with a decent sense of fairness. A few years back I was asked an unusual question as part of a lesson on self-interest. There is a red button. If I simply press the button (and I could do so as often as I liked) my pay will go up by 1%. The cost of my pay rise would be spread between the thousands of other employees in the firm. Would I press the button, perhaps even only a couple of times? In truth, I would probably press it until I had blisters on my finger even though I would like to think otherwise.

We get into trouble when we fail to recognise that incentives can *overly* focus our behaviour. Give a man a hammer and everything looks like a nail. Imagine the nature of a football game where the first goal scorer took all the spoils. There would be one hell of a scramble to score the first goal and it might make compelling viewing. The carrot is effective, but it is too pointed. We suddenly focus on the incentive and forget about the second order consequences. What we see is that narrow incentives influence performance, but they may not improve it. Studies of loan officer approvals during the recent US mortgage crisis showed that the loan officers actually believed the cases with the highest commission were more creditworthy. The effect was worse than naked self-interest: the incentive actually blinded their judgement.

Perverse Incentives

Understanding incentives is linked to second-level thinking. Many an incentive that was designed with a primary purpose in mind has backfired because the designers failed to consider what other interests might be affected, or how self-interest would manifest itself in a way that was contrary to what was expected. An example is monetary rewards offered to help exterminate unwanted animals such as rats and snakes. What authorities failed to foresee was that people would start to breed the rats and snakes. Forcing people to have overly complex passwords can be another perverse incentive. When faced with this complexity we simply write down our passwords somewhere "safe".

Incentives Are Not Just Monetary

Some people are "coin operated". But there really is much more to life than money. In one study, when people were offered cash to donate blood, the level of donations *decreased*. The money cheapened the nature of a charitable act where the true motivation was to feel good by doing good. In the modern workplace, money is only the housekeeping. What many of us really want is the chance to improve our skills, and, as writer Charles Handy put it, the canvas on which "to sign our own work". We aspire to have pride in what we do and to treat our work as our craft. We may be told the what and the why, but the *how* is up to us. Good incentives acknowledge recognition, public perception, and the value of pursuing work that we can be proud of. So yes, if we want to persuade, we should appeal to interests not reason. But when it comes to interests, appeal not just to net worth but also to self-worth.

Managing Incentives

On managing incentives there are two core principles worth remembering:

> We usually get the behaviour we reward; and
> It's mad to incentivise behaviour that we don't want.

Self-evident as these are, we routinely mess up the second, more often by errors of omission. Bureaucratic rules can develop in organisations to save people from making thoughtful decisions. So we end up with nonsense like: "You are correct, and I would love to help you, but our long-standing procedures don't allow it". What's more, if we build companies that have a culture of profit at all costs, we are doing our employees a grave injustice. Cartels, bribes and environmental damage all result from poor incentives. Considerable thought needs to be given to incentive design. Understanding the range and nature of interests involved is key. We should seek to design incentives to bring out the best in people and pay attention to actual behaviour as a warning alert for possible design flaws.

Incentives matter greatly – underestimate them at your peril. People will navigate the shortest path to the incentive. The curious among us will pay particular attention to incentives, monetary or otherwise.

Chapter Five:
Consider the Context

*There is no such thing as the view from
nowhere, or from everywhere for that matter.
Our point of view biases our observation,
consciously and unconsciously. You cannot
understand the view without the point of view.*
                                    - Noam Shpancer

When I was a teenager, I used to have arguments with a friend who refused to come to a firm view. His opinion was regularly couched in language like "it depends" or "we'll see". It drove me mad because I was much more likely to have a clear, black-or-white view. What I now realise is that I was quite likely to be wrong. Absolutes are rare birds. We should choose assessments over assertions.

Reassuringly Confident

Conviction is assuring. Western society places a high value on certainty. Bring us the single-handed advisors – those people who are confident, articulate and assured. Plain-spoken, firmly held views, are what count. Mark Twain quipped ironically that "all you need is ignorance and confidence and the success is sure". This is understandable as we need to be moving forward and conviction helps us do so. The problems begin when we extrapolate what worked in one set of circumstances to a different set of circumstances. We are prone to misjudge the behaviour of others when we don't fully consider the circumstances. If we are to be truly curious, we will carefully consider the context.

Context Dependency and Absence Blindness

Life is context-dependent. Scientists and statisticians understand this. They couch their conclusions in context-specific terms. Problems arise when people don't leave room for ambiguity. Dogmatic behaviour is especially worrying. Absolutism is dangerous. Very few "answers" are right in all circumstances. Even criminal judicial systems seek proof beyond a reasonable doubt, not absolute certainty.

A close cousin of context dependency is absence blindness. Humans are reasonably adept at examining and judging what is in front of them. We are excellent at comparing alternatives yet terrible at considering what's missing. Presented with a choice between A, B, C and D, we get very busy on the relative merits of each rather than suggesting a *context-appropriate* E. Out of sight, out of mind.

What's missing is also context-dependent. And if, like me, your head is beginning to hurt a little right now, that's because trying to consider both context relevance and what in that context we might be missing, does not come naturally. Understanding comes with consideration of both relevance and relevant absence.

A Thought Experiment

Carbon emissions are a real problem. Many cities are switching their carbon heavy diesel buses over to environmentally friendly electric buses. Is this a good thing? At face value, it seems so. But there are a lot of things we would need to know before we could have an informed opinion. We might want to start by qualifying the question: *For whom* is this a good thing? Other things we would like to know include whether the electricity powering the vehicles comes from a coal-fired electricity generation plant. Were the electric vehicles especially expensive to build and how were they funded? If funded by local government (and therefore ultimately by taxpayers), might there have been a more deserving use of that money? As you start to peel back the onion you will reveal lots of considerations. We are not simply seeking to explore whether electric vehicles are a good idea – we are seeking to understand when, where and in what circumstances we can be confident that they are desirable.

Economics author Henry Hazlitt neatly articulated context dependency and second level thinking in his single-sentence summary of economics: "The art of economics consists in looking not merely at the immediate but at the longer effects of any act or policy; it consists in tracing the consequences of that policy not merely for one group but for all groups."

The lateral thinking guru Edward de Bono used to posit that if you took a car and painted one side black and the other side white, crashed the car and then took eyewitness accounts of what happened you would learn a lot about the importance of perspective. We have different fields of view. This adds another dimension to context. It is not just overall factual context that matters, but *whose* context always needs to be considered, including whether they were working with the full picture (i.e. making allowance for what they didn't see).

Contextually Confident

Picture a confidence continuum as follows:

For most things, "contextually confident" seems like where we should be spending most of our time. Just because we are not certain doesn't mean we can't proceed. Things are always in flux, and we under-appreciate the role of luck or mere randomness, so we should never let the lack of certainty hold us back from getting on with things. Be assured, yet open-minded. A former work colleague's default setting was: "This is my opinion, and in this case I believe it to be the correct one." I didn't have a label at the time, but if I met him now I might say that he was contextually confident.

What are some practical suggestions for dealing with context dependency?

1. Always consider whether there is a better question.

2. Consider what might be missing.

3. For important decisions don't think twice, think thrice.

4. Use checklists.

5. Develop your own decision making frameworks and keep decision journals.

6. Think like a scientist would. The focus of the 'scientific method' is on empirical and measurable evidence.

7. Consult others who have real and relevant experience.

8. Widen the diversity of your own experience.

We can also be more careful and deliberate in our choice of words. "I know" is not the same as "I believe". Or, how about: "In my experience of similar situations, I have frequently found..."

Nothing occurs in isolation. Always consider the context and recognise that it: (a) is different for everyone, and (b) changes over time. Don't be dogmatic.

PART II
CHARACTER
(The Who)

Character: *Integrity and authenticity.*
Of good reputation. Principled.

We build character through our actions and our
motivations. Good choices are those that rest on
the foundation of good character.

Chapter Six:
Start by Considering the End
and the Opposite

> *Eleanor Rigby, died in the church*
> *And was buried along with her name*
> *Nobody came.*
>
> — Lennon & McCartney

Consider the End

To build a foundation of good character on which we can make good choices, we need to look forward. Start by considering the end. Why are we here and what do we hope to achieve? I guess, for most of us, life is about personal fulfilment of some sort or another. Yet we rarely ask ourselves what makes a fulfilling life. What does it look like? How would we describe it? What does it *feel* like? What would represent a great life? These are not easy questions and our answers may change over time.

Consider the Opposite

Some insight may be found by posing the opposite question: What might an *unfulfilled* life look like? Or worse, what would a truly wasted life look like? This approach of turning questions on their head is known as inversion. The dictum "Invert, always invert" is attributed to the German mathematician Jacobi. Inversion is a wonderful tool. To understand the nature of a life well lived, it is helpful first to consider the nature of a life that has been wasted.

Imagine that you have a significant birthday celebration coming up. A good friend is going to say a few words to mark your life thus far. What would you *not* like to hear? Do you feel a sinking feeling in your stomach? Imagining what you would *not* like to hear is pretty hard to do, because friends will always want to say *something* nice. The empty speech is the one where there is nothing distinctive to say about your life to date.

Let's be positive for a moment and think about what our celebration would look like in the case of a life well lived. Who is attending? What is the mood like? Is there a good sense of interest, not just with respect to your life thus far, but in what is yet to come?

I am currently in my late forties, an age where I am attending some of my friends' parents' funerals. The poignancy and beauty of the eulogies is always emotional. But why do we only say such nice things when someone is gone? It seems that funerals are for the living. Why not write now and let our loved ones know how much they matter to us?

The only thing we know for certain is that the final day eventually arrives for us all. How we live our life between now and then will be our story. What epitaph would we aspire to? What will the eulogy say? How would you like to be remembered? No one aspires to an empty eulogy.

This is not to say that we should dwell on death. Life is what we have. Life is where we dwell. In thinking about a life well lived we might ask whether we have maximised the best of what life has to offer. Is the world at least a slightly better place because of our presence? Have we made a positive difference? Greek philosophers encouraged eudemonia, which is broadly about being the best we can be.

In the pursuit of a life well lived, we are searching for what really matters to us personally and that is a deep exploration. Not many of us take the time to do this. One of the more visible exceptions is Ray Dalio. He is the founder of a highly successful investment firm called Bridgewater, and has crafted a very thoughtful set of principles. They are well articulated, comprehensive, and exceptionally logical, and you can find them online for free. At the risk of gross oversimplification one could summarise Dalio's suggested approach as:

1. Knowing what you want;
2. Knowing what's true;
3. Knowing what you need to do; and
4. Doing it.

Don't be fooled by how simple this looks. It is intuitive, practical and powerful.

Inversion More Widely
Beyond helping provide clarity on the lives we wish to avoid, inversion can be applied much more broadly. Anytime we are tackling an important project or decision, we can get more clarity when we invert. Try the following thought process:

1. What am I hoping to achieve? Look beyond the first level: What am I really looking to achieve? Don't just scratch the surface.

2. What does achievement look like to me? Express it in as much detail as possible.

3. What behaviour or actions would ensure that I *failed*?

4. What actions do I need to take to get to where I want to go (guided by avoiding the behaviours and actions in step 3)?

This is an elegant and deceptively effective way to tackle most things, large or small. To take a common practical example, let's say that you are doing an interview for a role that you really want. You can visualise what success looks like. Thinking about some of the things that will ensure that you fail to get the role (e.g. being late, unprepared, underdressed or unenthusiastic) can guide your planning.

Start by considering the end. Visualise both the road to personal fulfilment and the destination. Consider what behaviour would thwart that fulfilment and do the opposite. Thinking about the route to avoid helps reveal the more rewarding road.

Chapter Seven:
Emotional Intelligence

I want to know
if you can be alone
with yourself
and if you truly like
the company you keep
in the empty moments
- Extract from *The Invitation* by
Oriah Mountain Dreamer

If you were never a straight-A student, don't worry. There is a big difference between knowledge and intelligence. It is emotional intelligence, or emotional quotient (known as EQ), that helps us become rounded and grounded. How do we measure EQ? Much of the literature seeks to categorise it as follows: (i) self-awareness, (ii) self-regulation, (iii) empathy, (iv) social skills, and (v) motivation. I have instead tried to explore a wider list of traits to which we might aspire in our quest for greater emotional intelligence. Each trait could be considered a subset of one or more of the five categories, but I felt it would be helpful to widen our gaze.

Acceptance: It is what it is. You have probably heard of the *Serenity Prayer*, which owes its roots to stoic philosophers, in particular Epictetus: "God, grant me the serenity to accept the things I cannot change, courage to change the things I can, and the wisdom to know the difference." Nelson Mandela showed tremendous acceptance during his time in prison. So did Viktor Frankl in his time at a number of concentration camps.

Wishing that something which has already happened were different is pointless. "Would have, could have, should have" is waste of time and energy. This need not prevent us from learning from our mistakes. When we understand the value of acceptance, stress subsides. Acceptance is pragmatic. We can't change what has already happened, but we can choose our reaction.

Awareness: It is quite easy to go through life without thinking or reflecting. Busy fools on a thoughtless treadmill. Welsh poet W.H. Davies asked: "What is this life if, full of care, we have not time to stop and stare." People with high EQ tend to have a good feel for what is going on around them. They notice things. We might also call it perception – no bull (in the china shop).

Character: News media focus on how people look and what they have. By contrast, people with high EQ care more about who they are. Personality is peripheral but character is core. To be of strong character is one of the highest compliments. It is associated with trust, integrity and principles. We build character through integrity and authenticity. Choosing good role models also helps.

Communication: Communication is a key social skill. The interconnected world of non-face-to-face communication is a two-sided coin. Through technology we are theoretically more interconnected than ever, but the nature of our communication is evolving quickly and perhaps negatively. It is easy to misread words when they are taken in isolation from tone, facial expressions and body language. Good communicators are perceptive and tactful.

Compassion: Empathy has long been considered a highly desirable trait. But what good is it if I can feel your pain? Dr. Tania Singer at the Max Planck Institute and others have been researching the critical difference between empathy and compassion. Using advances in neuroscience, Singer's work has shown how compassion trumps empathy as a positive emotional trait. When people are compassionate they activate areas of the brain that *reduce* pain. The signature of compassion on the brain is a universally positive one. Think of how a mother cares for a sick child. She can show heartwarming love towards her child without experiencing the sickness. Health care workers with especially high levels of empathy can suffer high levels of burnout. At a societal level, it may be compassion that we should be seeking to encourage rather than empathy.

Equanimity: The Collins dictionary definition of *equanimity* is "calmness of mind or temper; composure". It derives from the Latin words *aequus* meaning "even" and *animus* meaning "mind". An even mind. The emotional part of our brain developed before the logical part. Sometimes we see red and can get into a fit of rage, for example if someone puts us down in public or threatens our self-esteem. Call it a mental mugging – where we fail to think before we act. The ability to keep the thinking brain in charge of the acting brain is the key to composure or temperance. It is what distinguishes humans from wild animals. Stay in control.

Honesty: Emotionally intelligent people are honest with themselves and with others.

Interdependence: We recently had a friend drop by to our house with his three-month-old daughter. To see this baby was a reminder of how *dependent* children are on their parents. As we grow older we strive for *independence*. But as we become more emotionally mature we begin to see interdependence as the highest form of human relations. Consider any typical day and contemplate the many people you relied on to go about your daily life. We are an intimate part of the human web of interdependence. How we are in the world has ripples farther than we can imagine. The minute we begin to celebrate being self-sufficient, we should check ourselves. No one is an island. Learning and accepting help from others creates value far beyond our individual capabilities.

Patience: The ability in young children to delay gratification is a strong indicator of success in later life. Nature teaches us this. The huge oak tree didn't spring up overnight. And neither do we. The flip side is that quite a lot can be achieved with time. We have all heard of the twenty year overnight success. An early mentor of mine used to say, "If you want to achieve anything in this life all you need is a clock on the leaning tower of Pisa" – the time and the inclination.

Perspective: Too far east is west, and too far west is east. We all have our own perspective. I simply can't know how you feel because I am not you. People with high EQ are awake to the multiplicity of different perspectives and possibilities. We already discussed the dangers of absolute thinking. Perspective comes from history and experience. How many of the world's problems and major conflicts today come from misunderstanding perspectives?

Resilience: We have just come through the worst financial crisis of our generation – the Great Recession. Large corporations have become especially focused on a particular personality trait, and that trait is resilience. This should not be a surprise to us. Resilience or grit gives us the capacity to treat setbacks as part of the forward journey, much like the way the pain of hard exercise helps us become fitter. Hardship is inevitable; it is how we deal with it that ultimately defines us. M. Scott Peck opens his classic book *The Road Less Travelled* with the line: "Life is difficult." It takes discipline and persistence to grow in this world. Flexibility is an important component of resilience.

Again we can look to nature for our analogies. The bamboo bends in the wind. It doesn't break.

Sociability: Emotionally intelligent people know how to both make and keep friends. This sociability is not the sole preserve of extroverts. Susan Cain, herself an introvert, raised the spirits of introverts worldwide with her thoughtful book, *Quiet*. Introverts are as sociable as extroverts, they just prefer to be sociable in smaller groups. Being loud and abrasive is not sociable. It is the opposite.

A combination of rational, conscious and respectful thinking is at the core of most traits associated with developing our emotional quotient. It is who and how we are that matters more than what we have and know.

Chapter Eight:
Fear

Gratitude looks to the past and love to the present: fear, avarice, lust and ambition look ahead.

- C.S. Lewis

Fear is deeply rooted in the human condition. One of the supposedly unique gifts of being human, our ability to contemplate how we will be in the future, may also be our greatest source of anguish. Fear has many faces and they are not pretty. Fear of loss, fear of death, fear of falling behind, fear of abandonment, fear of not being loved, fear of failure, fear of poverty, fear of commitment, fear of change, or fear of being found out for who we really are. The branches of fear are endless.

How we relate to fear says a lot about our character. We can be paralysed by fear. Or, we can take the time to understand fear and see it for the thought-based construct that it really is.

Fact-Based Fear and Thought-Based Fear
Fact-based fear occurs when you face a present and

immediate danger. You are walking home alone late at night when a menacing stranger threatens you with a knife. This is fact-based fear; it is real and your fight or flight defence mechanism will kick in. Our natural instincts are usually up to the task of dealing with immediate threats. At times of real threat we automatically summon extra strength, so the exploration of fact-based fear is not our current concern.

Then we have thought-based fear, which is another matter entirely. Here we are either worrying about the past or we are fearful for the future. It could be over something we did or didn't do. It could be over something that we are afraid might happen to us, or that might not happen to us. We all have our personal history and conditioning. Previous negative events can be replayed in our heads like horror movies being re-watched from our very own home video library. Yet the present moment, the only moment we ever have, is usually just fine. Any troubling fear is purely a thought-based construct. In fact, the vast majority of our fears are simply thought-based time distortions attempting to impose either the past or our fearful perception of the future on the present moment. When understood for the impostors that they truly are, our fears dissolve.

If you are invaded by thought-based fear, seek to recognise and *closely observe* the thoughts. Focus solely on the present moment. Ground yourself in the present moment where there is no harm – you are breathing and you are living. With practice, when we focus purely on the present moment we can face our fear, see it for the mental construct that it is, and watch it pass, like a cloud in the sky or a twig floating down a stream.

Fear of the Future

Fear of the future is also both thought-based and time-based. Everyone is afraid of something or other. The future is uncertain, and for many this is troubling. The most comfortable place an animal can be is in the middle of the herd. It feels safe and warm there. But when you think about it you realise that the view from the middle of the herd is not especially inviting.

Another helpful analogy is that of a ship. We are each the captain of our own ship. Fear of the future is the anchor that holds us in the harbour. Fear-ruled ships stay in safe harbours. But what use is a ship that won't set sail?

Fear is closely associated with anticipated loss. Change always brings the possibility of loss. The subtlety of loss is that it does not exist on its own. Loss must exist in relation to something, otherwise it has no meaning. We worry that we are losing out *as compared to* a present or perceived state. Comparison causes fear. Envy causes fear. Financier JP Morgan warned that nothing so undermines our judgement as the sight of our neighbours getting rich. All too often, our chosen scorecard is not an inner scorecard; it is an external comparative one, where we can never come out on top. The deep and difficult insight here is to stop comparing ourselves to others, to stop seeking to be "more than" others. Future fears melt away when we fully accept ourselves as we are, when we love ourselves, not in a narcissistic way, but in a compassionate way. If we drop our comparisons, our attachments and our demands we can then be free of fear. This is not to suggest that we don't look to develop skills, make friends or even accumulate things. They all have their place; we just need to ensure we don't derive our sense of self from them.

What about actual loss? We all experience loss. Loss is a natural part of life. Everything is transient, from the fruit fly to the great oak tree. The timescales may differ, but all things turn to dust eventually. We are going to be disappointed if we grasp too tightly. You might think that you are good-looking right now, and perhaps you are, but in thirty years' time you will be proclaiming that mirrors are not what they used to be! In recognising and accepting the impermanence of all things we choose awareness over attachment, flow over resistance. I think Alfred Tennyson had it right when he said it was better to have loved and lost than never to have loved at all.

Leaving the Harbour of Regret

In addition to understanding and accepting the natural inevitability of loss, there are a few other guideposts that can help coax us out of the harbour.

Firstly, we can cultivate a wide range of interests and relationships. It is dangerous to define ourselves by any single thing. Many workaholics have suffered disproportionately after losing their jobs. Many a loving spouse has not been able to recover from the loss of a partner. Whether it is a career, material wealth or a particular relationship, if we have defined ourselves by reference to one thing, our scaffolding falls apart if we lose it. We have no foundation to fall back on. A broad based, exploratory approach to life is more resilient to inevitable loss. Why linger on the loss when we can revel in the rebirth.

Secondly, when things go wrong, the consequences

are never as bad as our thought-based fears imagine them to be. Humans have an extraordinary capacity to adjust to circumstances, and numerous experiments have shown that we bounce back from difficulties far more easily than we think we will. This means we take far less risk than we should, based on the misjudged fear of how loss will impact us. If you have come through previous difficulties you will already appreciate this. The more you work through difficulties, the more able and inclined you are to keep stepping forward. Yes, we may get buffeted around occasionally, but we will be all the better for the buffeting. As the 13th century poet Rumi asked: "How will you ever be polished, if you are irritated by every rub?"

Thirdly, irrespective of what happens, we always have the capacity to choose our reaction. Our capacity to choose our response is evergreen and can't be taken from us. It is always with us, and from it we can draw great strength. Even in the horrors of a concentration camp, Viktor Frankl saw proof that "everything can be taken away from a man but one thing: the last of the human freedoms – to choose one's attitude in any given set of circumstances, to choose one's way". In the confines of the concentration camp, that ability to choose was clear in the most basic things, in the prisoners who comforted others, giving away their last piece of bread.

So yes, there will be loss. But we should know that:

- loss is natural and to be expected;
- the consequences of loss will not be as bad as we imagine, especially if we are living full and varied lives; and
- we never lose our capacity to learn, our capacity to love and, above all, our capacity to choose.

Our Choice

We have a choice right now.

Do we choose to face fear or do we choose regret?

Why not cast away the anchor of fear, leave the harbour of regret and let the winds of curiosity take us forth. Feet on the ground, eyes on the horizon...

Fear is mostly a thought-based construct. It dissolves when we drop our comparisons and accept ourselves fully as we are, right now. Loss is as natural as birth. Choose real life over regret.

Chapter Nine:
Know Yourself, Be Yourself,
Mind Yourself

> *I am not concerned with the driven or the*
> *sleepy mind but with one that is fully alert*
> *and free to express itself, for the mind shows*
> *its true nature only when it is free to play, free*
> *to be itself as fully as possible, just as a child*
> *will climb a tree under conditions of vigorous*
> *health, mental relaxation and the presence of*
> *an arboreal paradise.*
>
> - Extract from *Man's Emerging Mind*
> by N.J. Berrill

Know Yourself

Knowing ourselves is one of life's great challenges. "Above all, know thyself" is advice which has endured. It has stood the test of time for a reason. Knowing ourselves is fundamental.

But what does it mean to know yourself? How does one get to know oneself? What makes a person who he or she is? There is nature and nurture. All of us are born with a core personality which is the essence of who we are. As we grow we become conditioned by various factors around us. This conditioning comes primarily from the influences of our parents or primary care givers. Other people who have a strong influence on who we become include teachers, friends, peers and employers.

Why should we strive to know ourselves? The value of knowing ourselves permeates all aspects of our lives. How can we understand others if we first don't understand ourselves? Knowing ourselves gives context and clarity to the choices we make. Life is a series of choices; some are automatic (pulling your hand away from a hot object), others are conscious (choosing a meal at a restaurant). Many more are subconscious, like judgement. Our quality of life is heavily influenced by the quality of our choices. Knowing ourselves allows for more productive choices. It also helps with determination and resilience. If we understand why we choose a certain course of action we are more likely to see it through. Choice can also be one of inaction: the choice not to do something. Saying no is powerful when we clearly understand why we don't want to do something: "No, I won't work with that group of people because they have different values and different priorities to mine."

How do we get to know ourselves? Examining and reflecting on our feelings is one way. When someone makes us angry, sad, annoyed, bitter, jealous or joyful – our feelings are always about us rather than about the other person. Examined feelings are a treasure trove of personal understanding.

Asking lots of exploratory questions also helps. If you could pick three attributes to describe who you really are, what would they be? If you could pick three qualities to aspire to, what would they be? Is there any difference between your answers to who you are and who you aspire to be? Why? Try to come up with other thought-provoking questions to pose to yourself. It helps to consider extremes. When am I at my very best? When am I at my worst? Given the choice, who would I love to spend a lot of time with? Of the people I know well, who would I like to spend the least amount of time with? Why? What does that say about *me*?

Be Yourself

How many times have you been given this little nugget of advice? It is routinely dished out ahead of interviews, dates and new encounters: Just be yourself. But how does one "be oneself"? It is hard to be yourself if you don't know yourself, so knowing yourself is the first step. The second step is to accept yourself. So many of us have trouble accepting ourselves. We live in a culture that promotes the image of personal perfection – often with a perverse definition of perfection. There is more focus on having clean clothes than on having a clean conscience.

Strive to be yourself. In doing so, you might bear the following in mind:

- You are a unique being; cherish your individuality.
- No one is watching and monitoring you, at least to the degree that you might think.
- Not everyone will like you, and that's fine.

How can we be ourselves? Having personal goals and values is not a bad place to start. I work in an office and like to personalise it. I also have a habit – started some ten years ago – of designing my own notebook stationery that has a daily reminder of things that I find helpful to strive for. A few of the current aspirations are to:

- Ask questions, listen and understand.
- Stay positive, enthusiastic and considered.
- Foster trust-based relationships with people I respect.

This personal example might seem trivial to some. Who cares. The example is simply included to show that we can only be ourselves in our own way. The real trouble comes when we start to act on other people's expectations of us, or on our misguided interpretation of other people's expectations.

You might be concerned that being yourself will cause people to stereotype you as odd or eccentric. Fear not. Edinburgh scientist David Weeks has studied the links between eccentricity and well-being. In his wonderful book *Eccentrics: A Study of Sanity and Strangeness*, Weeks shows that because eccentrics worry less about what others think of them, they are often *less* prone to stress and other medical ailments. Those we label as eccentrics demonstrate higher levels of curiosity, humour and creativity.

I can still remember my Dad saying to me, "If your sister put her hand in the fire, would you do it too?" You may remember similar admonishments yourself, designed to protect you from peer pressure. Always think for yourself. Don't automatically accept what you are told. This independence can be difficult as we are social animals and we want to blend in with our friends – it's an innate desire. People do things because that's what they observe others doing. As a historical survival mechanism this observation of others was useful, and at times invaluable. If everyone is running in the opposite direction, at speed, chances are it is for a good reason. It may indeed be wise to run first and ask questions later. Better to miss lunch than to be lunch.

But here's the problem. Mimicking others can lead to all sorts of difficulties, some small, but others utterly tragic. A particularly stark example is that of the Kaulong people, chronicled by Jared Diamond in his book *The World Until Yesterday*. Up until as recently as circa 1957, the Kaulong people (a small population east of New Guinea), had a practice of strangling anyone who became a widow. This barbarous act was done by the widow's brother or one of her sons. Why was it done? We will never know for sure, but "tradition" probably played a part.

Being yourself doesn't mean being stubborn. Calling someone "his own man" or "her own woman" can be interpreted as accusing someone of being difficult or single-minded. It may be better instead to think of them as being happy in their own skin. Not trying to be someone else.

Everyone is unique for good reason. Embrace your uniqueness. Nothing in this world is perfect, and at the same time everything is. Leonard Cohen states this beautifully in his song "Anthem":

> *There is a crack in everything,*
> *That's how the light gets in.*

Let the light in and be happy with who is revealed.

Mind Yourself

Some things can't be delegated. Minding yourself is one such thing.

In an aircraft emergency, put on your own oxygen mask first. You can't help others if you are not well. We have all seen mothers caring for others while neglecting their own well-being.

Our well-being comes in two parts, physical and mental. You can find ample good advice on physical health. Physical well-being is largely determined by the right combination of nutrition, sleep and exercise. Rest is crucial. Tiredness is responsible for many of our mistakes.

Mental health is more complex. Maintaining our self-esteem is critical. Fundamentally this is about loving ourselves unconditionally – compassionately recognising our core humanity and capacity to make our own way. Poor mental health is destructive. Whether it is a general unease, anxiety or depression, poor mental health is debilitating. I suspect that most of us will have someone in our circle of friends or family who has battled with mental anxiety, or will have met with such mental pain ourselves. About one in four of us gets an unwelcome visit from the "black dog" at some point in our lives. It is a frightening and horrible experience that is completely alien to people in good mental health.

It is not easy to vanquish the anguish. A lot depends on our upbringing. Difficult upbringings make us more susceptible to mental anxiety later in life so it may be out of our control to prevent. That said, if we would like to reduce the risk of mental anxiety the following may be helpful:

1. Pursue a purpose. The late self-help writer Stephen Covey encouraged us to Live, Love, Learn and Leave a Legacy.

2. Aim for a balance between work and play. Extremes of either are harmful over prolonged periods.

3. Rest. Take time out and switch off the noisy mental chatter. Look at the beauty and stillness in nature without trying to analyse it, or listen to relaxing music without trying to 'do' or 'achieve' anything else at the same time.

4. Practise accepting what is. What angers us controls us. Stress comes from wrestling with reality.

5. Stand up for yourself. You have the basic right to be treated with respect and dignity.

6. Believe in something bigger than yourself.

Know yourself and see the journey. Be yourself and enjoy the journey. Mind yourself and extend the journey.

Chapter Ten:
Be Kind to Your Parents

*Be kind, for everyone you meet
is fighting a harder battle.*

- Plato

Our tendency to return favours seems to have a good degree of proportionality to it. Dinner at our place in return for dinner at our friends' house. A helping hand with a house move. A thoughtful birthday present. An eye for an eye. The proportionality of reciprocity.

But there is a slightly worrying exception. We can feel a lesser sense of proportionality towards those closest to us.

How should twenty years of caring be reciprocated?

They say a mother's work is never done and most of us have witnessed the wide reach of a mother's compassion. The discomfort of pregnancy. The pain of childbirth. Years of sleepless nights. Daily care. Endless worrying. Unconditional love.

Women seem to be better than men when it

comes to caring for their parents. My wife recounted how a friend of hers had been caring for her mother. She had been spending a huge amount of time and effort looking after her mum. It looked like a considerable inconvenience. When my wife complimented her she replied: "It is no work at all, in fact it is a *privilege* to be able to care for my mum." What a great mindset.

You don't have to wait until your mother is old before you are kind to her. There are lots of ways to show gratitude. Showing appreciation, spending time together and making small gestures of kindness are all that is required. Her first concern is that you are OK. So do her a favour, know yourself, be yourself and mind yourself. Occasionally ask for her advice and listen thoughtfully. Consider a handwritten letter. Explain in your own words why you are grateful for everything your mother has done and continues to do for you. She will treasure that.

I never got to write a letter to my mum. We had so little time together. Her name was Eileen and she died when I was thirteen.

My dad had to be the mother and father in our house. Thanks, Dad. Some kindness is coming your way.

Kindness is not just for strangers.

Chapter Eleven:
Sales, Negotiation and Influence

I have always said that everyone is in sales.
Maybe you don't hold the title of salesperson,
but if the business you are in requires you to
deal with people, you, my friend, are in sales.
                                    - Zig Ziglar

What are the first few thoughts that spring to mind when I mention *sales*? Are you thinking pushy, slick characters, used cars, shiny suits or some other less than endearing label? To say someone is a good salesman or saleswoman is not necessarily a compliment. Why is that? Why do we get a tiny bit uncomfortable when we think of sales? Our reaction is driven by stereotypes. We think of a good salesperson as someone who convinces us to buy something that we don't really need. We are duped by false charm. While the stereotype exists, it is an exaggeration and it misses a fundamental truth. The truth is that we are all sales people. Yes – *you* are a salesperson. Sales skills are a natural part of who we are and how we interact with the world.

We may not realise it but we are all natural born sellers. Remember how we used to get our way as a child? Our abilities may vary, but this doesn't take from the fact that sales is an everyday endeavour. Think back to a first date where you probably demonstrated some skills in selling your best personality traits. Or simply look back on how you spent the last month and think about how much of your time involved "selling" – for example in the form of looking to have your views heard.

The vast majority of people are happy to get by using only their natural skills, which improve over time through learning from experience. But there is something important that most of us don't learn early enough in life, if at all. There is a science to selling. Understanding the science can help us become far more effective sellers.

Beyond our narrow, traditional view of sales there is a broader view. Think about a typical week. You might want to invite a friend to go to the movies with you – with a preferred movie, place or time in mind. Or you may be making the case for a new hire, seeking funding for a project or raising money for charity – all are a form of selling. What about choosing a holiday destination? You want relaxation and your friend prefers to visit tourist attractions. Or perhaps you are simply trying to persuade someone to try something new? So beyond our narrow view of sales there is a much wider sales sphere. This wider sphere comprises sales, negotiation and influence. Our natural abilities are enhanced by understanding the science.

The Science of Selling
(or why "Friends Fish with Fearless Frank")

(i) Friends. A number of years ago I was managing a company and looking to hire a head of sales. What I didn't fully appreciate at the time was that the CEO is really the head of sales in every company, at least in the broadest sense. Leaving my personal blind spot aside, I continued my search for the right salesperson. When meeting candidates I took every opportunity to ask them what in their view makes a great salesperson. The best answer I got was from a young man who had built his career in some of the most hostile and least developed regions of the world. He told me that "sales is about making friends with people on the ground". He innately understood that people like doing business with people whom they like and trust. If you want to increase your sales, make more friends. The "on-the-ground" part of the response was also insightful. As with many things, half of success is about showing up – and that means face-to-face.

(ii) Fish. Where is the best place to fish? Where the fish are. If you are going to sell, you may as well spend your time with those who are most likely to want to buy. Leave the long shots to others. One of my early mentors used to advise me to "find the MAN", explaining that if I wanted to get a positive response I needed to speak to someone with the Money, the Authority and the Need to buy from me.

(iii) Fearless. The best salespeople see rejection as a way to learn, improve and work towards mastery of their profession. Resilience allows the fearless salesperson

to accumulate many rejections without losing sight of the bigger picture. They have no fear of failure.

(iv) Frank. To make an honest sale you need to believe in yourself, and you need to believe in your product or service. You must genuinely believe that you are helping someone do what is right for them. Not selling, but helping people to buy. Getting to the position where you honestly believe that you have the right solution requires both preparation and a thorough understanding of the needs of the person you are trying to serve. To sum up, we can be frank when we bring honesty and belief to our thoughtful preparation.

The Science of Negotiation

Just as with innate sales skills, we all have some natural negotiation skills. With a chocolate bar firmly in her grasp, the screaming three-year-old girl in the supermarket is trading off her parents' embarrassment against her total lack of embarrassment. While this may be an effective negotiating strategy in that situation, it is unlikely to be effective when the child is back at home.

As adults we have preconceived ideas about negotiating. For example, we are happy to negotiate when buying a new car, but highly reluctant to do so when buying our groceries at the local supermarket. A negotiation occurs any time there is a possible exchange between parties and both parties have a choice *not* to make the exchange. Unless both parties have an alternative (or at least perceive that to be the case), it is not a negotiation.

A lot has been written about negotiation and there

are many theories, some conflicting. My assumption is that we are negotiating with someone with whom we want to have a continuing relationship or may meet again at some stage in the future (which should be our working assumption). I have tried to capture the essence of the science in ten traits of successful negotiators which are listed below.

1. Successful negotiators prepare. They have very clear goals. In getting from A to B they understand the scale of the journey, the terrain and as many of the routes and modes of transport as possible. They seek to understand the terrain for *both* parties, not just their own. They know what their "best" and "walk away" options are, and they have a view on the corresponding options of the other party.

2. Successful negotiators seek bigger pies, not bigger slices. The "limited pie" mentality is small-minded. In the "limited pie" world your gain is my loss and vice-versa – it's a zero-sum game. By collaborating there are invariably ways for both parties to share in a much larger pie. Collaborate, don't compete.

3. Successful negotiators take their time. Time is your friend. You never want to be rushed, because the temptation is to accept less than a fair deal. Watch out for false deadlines. They can be abused to push you into a poor outcome.

4. Successful negotiators focus on understanding the underlying <u>interests</u> of both parties. They distinguish between stated positions and underlying motivations.

This requires a questioning mindset, a desire to get beneath the surface or under the bonnet. What is really motivating both parties? What are the real needs, and are there other ways of satisfying those real needs? If what the other party is suggesting doesn't make sense, good negotiators don't reject it, they reframe it.

5. Successful negotiators understand perception. A line sometimes attributed to Mark Twain goes: "Never let the truth get in the way of a good story." The equivalent in negotiation is never let the facts get in the way of a fair outcome. The simple truth is that we have different perceptions of "facts". We are emotional beings, and negotiations are an emotional engagement. Our goal is to satisfy both parties' real needs. How *you* perceive the other person's real needs is irrelevant. What matters is how *they* perceive them. What pictures are in their heads and how are you going to paint a picture that works for them?

6. Successful negotiators maximise, but never overuse, their perceived power. We maximise our perceived power through: (i) having other options (i.e. not having to do this particular deal), (ii) understanding the nature of alternative solutions, (iii) a willingness to invest or commit resources, (iv) expertise, (v) third-party legitimacy, and (vi) our demeanour. Be relaxed, firm, patient and cooperative.

7. Successful negotiators rarely ever accept the first offer. Why? Because by doing so the other person feels bad. They feel foolish. So even if the first offer is better than your original best case expectations, find a way to curb your enthusiasm and seek some improvement. It can be around related items. For example if you are being offered a starting salary that is better than you hoped, it may be wise to counter with a request for some additional training days, flexible hours or your next salary review within a six month period rather than the standard twelve. Now if you are thinking of all those first offers that you accepted previously, don't despair, as in some cases it may not have been a negotiation. Those cases are rare however and the best negotiators understand that too.

8. Successful negotiators believe that virtually everything is negotiable. Remember the grocery example earlier. Why don't we negotiate in the grocery store? Two reasons. Firstly it is not customary and secondly the people at the tills have not usually been given the authority to negotiate. On customs, as with policies and procedures, great negotiators know that anything that is designed by people can be changed by people. The "standard contract" is a ploy to force people into the sheep pen. There are always exceptions, and simply asking whether there have *ever* been any exceptions can usually foil the policies and procedures ploy. On the authority point, the best negotiators simply ask to speak to the people with the authority. For example, if you have been held up for an unreasonably long time in the shopping queue you might demand to see the manager and say: "I like shopping here and hope to come back, but today's wait was very frustrating. What can you do to make up for my inconvenience?"

9. Successful negotiators delve into differences. Differences are a treasure trove of differing perceptions of value. People don't value the same things in the same way. By trading things of different perceived value, we increase the pie. For example, we can give someone a deserved positive reference or introduction. This is virtually free to give but of large value to the other party.

10. Successful negotiators incrementally and continually build on common ground. They constantly summarise what is agreed as the negotiations proceed, building brick by brick, towards a collaborative negotiated outcome. This slowly builds trust, and trust is the essential ingredient of successful negotiations. The cynical negotiator refers to this stratagem as "salami-slicing" and an experienced customer will set out his bargaining position as "nothing is agreed until everything is agreed".

While the science of negotiation tends to be associated with specific transactions, the science of influence is more broad based.

The Science of Influence

When it comes to the topic of influence the best thing I can do for readers is to suggest they read Cialdini's *Influence: The Psychology of Persuasion*. In his enlightening book, Cialdini introduces six principles of influence. The principles are very firmly grounded in human psychology.

Principle One: Reciprocation. When you give something to someone they feel obliged to give something back in return. If you want to receive, give first. The best salespeople use this all the time. They give value first.

Principle Two: Scarcity. People want what's scarce. You should emphasise genuine scarcity whether in the form of unique features or limited editions. The luxury goods market is built on the foundations of scarcity. The diamond market is built on perceived scarcity.

Principle Three: Social Proof or Consensus. We are social animals. People do things if other people are doing them. Seeing people similar to us (or people we aspire to be like) promote products makes us think, "If it's good for them, it must be good for us." Books, songs and movies reach tipping points where people buy them because everyone else is buying them.

Principle Four: Authority. We have a psychological tendency to respect authority. This causes us to buy all sorts of "scientifically proven" products.

Principle Five: Consistency. Being inconsistent is considered undesirable. We go to great lengths to avoid inconsistency. Therefore to influence behaviour it is best to start from a common understanding and build slowly from there. Build on existing commitments. A powerful question in keeping someone to a commitment is: "Do I have your word on it?"

Principle Six: Liking. We are far more likely to be influenced by our friends. If you want to increase your influence with someone else, strengthen your friendship with them.

An Additional Ingredient
Those of good character add a critical further ingredient to their natural ability and their understanding of the science. That ingredient is integrity.

> *Good Character = Principled Sellers =*
> *Natural Ability + Science + Integrity*

Principled sellers only sell a product or service that they believe in. They need to believe in themselves, their product or service and the company they represent. They would not seek to persuade others to do anything they would not do themselves, were the roles reversed.

A principled seller should give people the same respect, service and care that they would reserve for a close relative, recognising that there is no limit to the quality one can add to a service. How might we distinguish the principled seller from the unsavoury one? One possible question: Would you sell this to your mother, assuming she had the need?

Sales, negotiation and influence are an essential part of our daily dealings with friends, associates and the world at large. We all have natural abilities that can be enhanced through experience and through understanding the science. People of good character exercise their skills with integrity.

Chapter Twelve:
Adversity

As soon as there is life there is danger.
- Ralph Waldo Emerson

S ometimes life just throws muck in your face. Imagine you are a hard-working, good-natured single parent who wakes up one morning to find that your car has been stolen. Rushing to catch a taxi you trip, tear your new suit, and end up being late for a sales meeting which costs you an important client. To cap it off, you learn later that day that your company is downsizing and that you are being laid off. With three young children to care for, you wonder how you are going to cope. But you do cope.

Adversity is both inevitable and relative. Everyone meets with adversity, but not in equal measure. Nor do we respond in the same way. Many of us have a tendency to sweat the small stuff and get troubled by trivialities. Meanwhile, some people take adversity in their stride. Take Kyle Maynard. The moment Kyle was born he was whisked away from his parents by the doctors. His worried parents were soon to learn that he was born with a condition known as congenital amputation – he had stumps for arms and legs. Before school Kyle was fitted with prosthetics but asked his mother to get rid of them because they impeded his ability to get down on the ground and play with other kids. His mother obliged and Kyle could again play, unstilted and uninhibited, the way other kids do. He took up football at age eleven and later wrestling. Apparently Kyle is fond of saying: "I know what I can do, and I'm going to do it", not in a boastful manner, but with a singular focus on the art of the possible. In 2012 he became the first quadruple amputee to scale Mount Kilimanjaro. You can read about Kyle's life in his autobiography: *No Excuses: The True Story of a Congenital Amputee Who Became a Champion in Wrestling and in Life*.

Another person who has admirably handled adversity is Joanne O'Riordan. Joanne doesn't have any limbs either and you can watch her tell her story in an October 2012 Ted Talk entitled *No Limbs, No Limits*. It is a story of bravery, curiosity and tenacity. It is also a reminder of the very special power of a family that cares for each other.

Why do some people cope better than others when faced with adversity? Or consider a better question: How can we cope with adversity and perhaps even grow through adversity? I think there are three things that can help:

> *Reflection* on the nature of adversity, with a view to understanding;

> *Recognition* of when we personally face adversity, with a view to acceptance; and

Re-writing our life story to account for the experience of adversity, with a view to personal growth.

Through *reflection* we seek to understand the nature of adversity, for what is understood is less frightening when it arrives. Primarily, we learn that adversity is a natural part of life. It is naive to assume that it doesn't exist, or that we won't be hit by adversity's arrow. When we observe the world around us, we see how much suffering people frequently deal with. Adversity can entail premature or disproportionate loss. We may lose a parent, but if they have lived a long life we can accept their passing, sad as it is. But a parent losing a child, that's another matter entirely, and probably one of the most difficult and cruel things for anyone to have to face. There is also the traumatic suffering where children are abused, neglected, abandoned or abducted – a suffering that words could never describe. Some people are dealt a disproportionate amount of pain. Adversity is distributed neither in equal measure nor with reason. Bad things can and do happen to good people. The purpose of reflecting on adversity is to understand that it is inevitable, indiscriminate and arbitrary.

Through reflection and research we may also find role models like Kyle, Joanne and the countless others who, somehow, find growth through adversity. Reflecting on the lives of people who suffer trauma in a wide array of circumstances can help put our own trials in perspective. There is no shortage of material from the devastation of wars, natural disasters, chronic illness, to the horrors of homicide, suicide and genocide. And as we have already observed, we often don't need to look too far from home to witness adversity. Understanding the nature of adversity may make us more compassionate when we notice it in others.

It was German philosopher Friedrich Wilhelm Nietzsche who observed that what didn't kill him made him stronger. Though Nietzsche speaks a real truth, we should be mindful that severe trauma hurts deeply. We would not wish it on anyone. It is easier to grow following medium levels of adversity than it is to grow following severe trauma – some pain may simply be too extreme to be a growth catalyst. So I am not going to romanticise adversity. If I were given a magic wand and could choose whether my children face adversity in life, I would choose some, but not too much. We can learn a lot from the university of adversity. But again, let's not be hostage to fortune, and instead count our blessings if we have managed to dodge the arrows in the shadows.

Through *recognition* our goal is to truly face adversity when we come in contact with it, and not avoid it. A frequent reaction to adversity is to deny it happened. For example people often seek to avoid recognising what happened through alcohol or drugs. When we are hit by adversity it helps to ask ourselves: What is life expecting of me now? Adversity places a fork in the road. Our previous assumptions about the way the world works and our place in it may need to be revised. Faced with this new fork in the road we can choose to take the high road or the low road. The low road appears easier, but it is downhill. It is the road of avoidance, social withdrawal, blaming, brooding, distraction and anger. The high road is harder, it is uphill, but the view from the top is clearer. Unlike the lonely low road where we tend to go it alone, on the high road we are accompanied by friends or professional helpers. The high road is the road of acceptance, awareness, perspective and perseverance.

In *re-writing* we are tasked with updating our life story to incorporate the adversarial event. How we see ourselves and how we feel about ourselves are tightly bound with the life story we tell ourselves. The personal narrative that we attribute to adversity can have a tremendous impact on how we move on. A "victim narrative" can take us under, but a "survivor narrative" helps us to cope. Some go beyond a "survivor narrative" and take on a "growth narrative". Through a "growth narrative" we are interpreting adversarial events as an opportunity to demonstrate our resilience, choose our response and take ownership of our future. Growth is an endless quest, set always against the benchmark of our previous self. Frequently the "growth narrative" leads to a greater focus on relationships, experiences, learning, community service and a fresh appreciation of what it means to be alive.

Adversity does not discriminate. We can't avoid it — all we can do is seek to understand it and when we ultimately meet it recognise the question it is asking of us. The answer to that question is within us and no one else.

Chapter Thirteen:
Be a True Friend

Oh, the comfort, the inexpressible comfort,
of feeling safe with a person, having neither
to weigh thought nor measure words, but to
pour them all right out, just as they are, chaff
and grain together, knowing that a faithful
hand will take and sift them, keep what is
worth keeping, and then, with a breath of
kindness, blow the rest away.

- George Eliot
(pen name of Mary Ann Evans)

Friendship is the thread that binds the fabric of humanity. Do you have some true friends? Who are they?
Who would you feel comfortable calling at 4am, explaining that you needed their help in an emergency? Who could you call upon to mind your two dogs for a few weeks while you went to hospital for an operation? Who could you rely upon if you were in trouble? Your answers may give you some clues as to who your true friends are. You may find

that family members feature prominently.

How many *non-family* friends could you rely on in a time of need? If there is one – or, even better, a few – then you have something to truly treasure.

Now, think a little more deeply and ask yourself this: How many of those people would call you if the tables were turned? To have true friends, you need to be a true friend.

Cultivating friendships is an extremely important life pursuit. The benefits of strong friendship networks to health, happiness and longevity are well recognised. Choose your friends wisely as they can contribute greatly to who you become. I recall my grandmother saying, "Show me your friends and I'll tell you who you are."

Friendship comes in many forms. Women tend to relate to each other in emotionally supportive face-to-face dialogue. Men, by contrast, tend to relate by doing things together – side by side. These are generalisations, of course, but not overly so.

There is also the special case of kinship. We get to choose our friends but not our family. Sibling rivalry can be worse than the rivalry between strangers. This is a tragedy. We spend a very long time with our family, especially our siblings if we are lucky enough to have them. The bonds of brotherly and sisterly love can be the greatest gift of all. Roman philosopher Gaius Musonius Rufus had this to say: "How much better it is to have many brothers than to have many possessions. This is because possessions invite plots from neighbours, and brothers forestall these plotters."

How else might we think about the nature of true friendship?

A true friend:

- Won't lie to protect your feelings, but speaks the truth lovingly and gently.

- Won't judge whether what you're feeling is right or wrong, instead encouraging you to discover your own truth.

- Will keep you from becoming your own worst enemy.

- Will celebrate your personal victories with the same excitement as they would their own.

- Will help you find your own path in life, even if it takes you in the opposite direction to theirs.

- Accepts you for who you are and doesn't seek to change this.

- Forgives you, because they understand the bigger picture.

- Expects nothing from you, but wants everything for you.

- Is always there, even if you have forgotten them for a while.

It is said that a dog is a man's best friend. I didn't really understand this until I *experienced* it. We have two dogs, Wilbur and Skye. Every time I return from being out of the house, I am greeted with a delightfully warm dog welcome.

By contrast, strangers can appear cold. Though let's not forget William Butler Yeats' claim that strangers are simply friends who have not yet met. True friends are warm. Warmth is more powerful than force. One of Aesop's fables recounts a contest between the strong winds and the warm sun – each arguing that they were more powerful than the other. They decided that the victor would be determined by who could persuade a passing stranger to take off his coat. The harder the wind blew the more the man clung to his jacket. All the sun had to do was suddenly shine with all its warmth. Warmth works wonders.

Friends are warm.

Consider being **WARM** as a reminder to be:

Welcoming – When we see our friends we instinctively make them feel welcome with a smile and a warm greeting. Friends don't need to make appointments. Indeed we can be even more welcoming of a surprise visit.

Authentic – Friends are free to be themselves. And friends allow us to be ourselves.

Reliable – Friendship requires effort. We may not always be in the mood to spend time with our friends, or to help them, but we do it anyway. Friends are reliably there for each other. Time is no barrier to friendship. No matter how much time has passed when we meet up with old friends, it feels like time falls away and we reignite with that part of us that liked each other from the start.

Mutually Respectful – There is no friendship without mutual respect. In a balanced relationship, each friend respects the other for who they are.

To be a true friend is the greatest gift you can give and receive.

Chapter Fourteen:
Simplicity

Speak your truth quietly and clearly
                                    - From *Desiderata*

E ven though the universe is vast, complex and ambiguous we find beauty in simplicity. There is no need to overcomplicate things. People who can express themselves clearly, demonstrate real understanding and are more likely to be taken seriously. Credibility and clarity go hand in glove. We should be clear in our communication, both written and oral. If something does not have to be long and complex, then short and sweet is the way to go.

We are seeing an increasing use of complex language as a cloak of intelligence, when in fact the opposite is more often the case. Pretentious writing is not a demonstration of intelligence. I have nothing against elaborate writing or speech but we need to ask: Is it necessary? There are many ways of saying things. Instead of saying "at this point in time", perhaps "now" is sufficient. Or we may ask someone whether they are experiencing discomfort or pain when a simple "does it hurt?" would suffice.

Edward de Bono said that complexity is failed simplicity. We get busy training people to deal with complexity when we should be seeking to simplify.

Simplicity is elegant.

Complexity brings us conspiracy theories and over-elaborate explanations for natural occurrences. Clever minds come up with intricate explanations which are more about showcasing their "knowledge" than arriving at the most reasonable explanation. To counteract this tendency many have sensibly invoked what's known as Occam's razor, a scientific rule of thumb that urges us to first consider the possible solution with the least number of assumptions. The more obvious explanation is usually the better *starting* point.

We also see the English language getting butchered in a deliberate attempt *not* to call a spade a spade. For the last eight years *Financial Times* columnist Lucy Kellaway has presented "corporate guff" awards. In Lucy's 2013 *Golden Flannel Awards* two categories were especially amusing. On corporate executives using different words for *fired* we got: *demised, transitioned out of the company, disestablished* and *completed*. And for new forms of *communicating with people* we got: *loop me in, let's connect*, and even *inbox me*. There was also a lot of reaching – *reach out, reach down,* and *reach around*. I'm not sure whether we should be reaching or retching. In an engineering context, W.B. Stout, a Ford Motor Co. executive, had a memorable phrase: "Simplicate and add more lightness".

On building character our preference should be to speak and write clearly. The ability to reduce something to its essence is the true mark of understanding. Be wary of complexity for complexity's sake.

See above...

PART III
CHOICE
(The What)

Choice: *The act of choosing or selecting.*

Our ability to choose is one of life's great gifts. We are the product of our choices. Good choices come from good character, and a few good choices make all the difference.

Chapter Fifteen:
Choosing a Career

Nice work if you can get it.
And you can get it if you try.

- Ira Gershwin

Headwork not Footwork
Work smarter not harder. What does that mean? There is an implicit suggestion that work is hard and smart is easy. If smart were easy we would all be at it. It's not. Being smart requires us to think long and hard about what *really* matters, understanding what we value most. This chapter is about choosing a career that can give us the best opportunity for both monetary and non-monetary reward. An underappreciated aspect of life is that rewards received are not directly proportional to effort expended. Understanding that principle early in life will make a meaningful difference to your quality of life.

Work you Enjoy
Do what you love and love what you do. If you work at what you enjoy, it won't feel like work. Being "in

the zone" is not work: we are fully engaged and don't notice time passing. Too often people do what their parents want them to do, what their friends encourage them to do, or indeed what they feel they *should* do, given their life influences or financial situation. It is a tragedy to see people wasting their potential and passion on what others think is "good". Finding a career that you enjoy is one of the most valuable things you can do in life. Imagine getting paid to do what you really enjoy doing anyway?

Working at something that we enjoy should be a fundamental objective for all of us. Simply don't compromise on this. I appreciate that life's necessities have a nasty habit of getting in the way at times. We frequently need to work just to pay the bills. When this is the case then at least try to work in an area that moves you towards working at what you enjoy. It will be easier knowing that you are moving in the right direction.

Finding what you enjoy may require some experimentation. So experiment. What you enjoy may change over time. Don't fear change, befriend it, for change is inevitable. If your work or career is not right for you, then change represents the only way to bring you closer to what you truly enjoy. Let the long-term prize of enjoyable work give you the strength to handle the short-term discomfort of change.

People speak of *finding* their passion. I think the more appropriate advice is to pursue your passion, as your passion will naturally emerge when you gradually figure out (a) what you enjoy doing, and (b) what you are good at.

Share of Value

When I talk about share of value I am referring to sharing in the profits of your employer's enterprise. Broadly speaking there are two types of monetary reward system. Reward System A is what could be categorised as "power by the hour" where monetary rewards are broadly proportional to the number of hours we put in. Think of employees who get paid a particular rate per hour. I think of Reward System A as representing *footwork*, as the reward is largely proportional to the number of hours worked. To walk ten miles you must take a set number of steps. You can improve your speed, productivity or fitness, but fundamentally there are limits to improvement, and therefore monetary rewards are capped. As there are only so many hours in a week, you are capping your financial potential. Most employees work largely in the realm of Reward System A, that is, *footwork*.

By contrast, Reward System B is categorised by what I call "share of value" or *headwork*. In this category financial rewards are in some way proportional to the value created. Think of business owners, entertainers, commission-based salespeople, entrepreneurs, and those careers that offer profit participation (e.g., through bonus pools or share options). You may know people who were granted shares in their company and now those shares are quite valuable. These people may have a total compensation significantly greater than yours even though they work no harder than you.

If you are lucky enough to find yourself in a "share of value" situation, it may be helpful to study the 80/20 principle, which posits that output is not proportionate to input, or value to effort. Let's say that 20% of a firm's employees are delivering 80% of its profits. As an employee of that firm you can be in the 20% category that delivers the 80%, or the 80% category that delivers the 20%. There are no prizes for guessing which category you should aspire to belong to. But what you may not fully appreciate is the degree of difference between those two categories. The higher-value category is an astonishing sixteen times more productive than the lower-value category. If you are an employee in the higher value category, you are in a stronger negotiating position for sharing in value creation.

None of this is to suggest that financial reward should be our primary goal when choosing a career. Vocations and volunteers put serving society ahead of financial gain, yet achieve immeasurable personal satisfaction. Doing what we enjoy is far more important than crass cash. But why not strive for both? Harnessing the power of sharing in value can be substantially more financially rewarding when compared to areas where wages are capped – for the *same* effort.

Work With People whom You Trust and Respect
We need to do our homework on the people with whom we choose to work. If we find people whom we trust and respect, we should move heaven and earth to get on board with them, especially if we can find a good mentor. I have been fortunate to have had some excellent mentors, and was especially lucky to have had a great mentor very early in my career.

In choosing a career the most important thing is to pursue work that we enjoy. We get to career utopia if we can also share in value creation and work with people we respect and trust.

Chapter Sixteen:
The Ubiquity of Energy

> *If you want to find the secrets of the universe, think in terms of energy, frequency and vibration.*
>
> - Nikola Tesla

Nothing happens without energy. Everything that is produced requires the application of energy. The same goes for us as individuals. The application of energy can be good or bad. Consider the humble matchstick. It can be used to light a candle during an electricity blackout or it can spark a fatal fire.

As a young schoolboy I had a brief obsession with burning objects while they were on metal weighing scales, curiously watching weight turn to heat without understanding the science of the matter. My physics teacher banished me to a concrete open area in the school grounds where I could experiment in *relative* safety.

The discovery, and more importantly *control*, of energy in the form of fire was a critical progress point for humanity. Think of the early benefits of light, heat and cooked meat. Or later on, when iron was made into tools. The world's technological progress owes its existence to the *controlled application* of energy. All living things are in a continuous battle for energy. Why do animals eat each other? For energy. Humans fight over drilling rights for energy and ultimately profit. The geopolitics of oil and gas are testament to the critical importance of energy.

As living beings we consume and continuously convert energy. Our brains are heavy users. The quality of our calorific intake is important to our health, as is how we store energy and how our body and our organs use it. And while all of these factors are important, when it comes to getting the most from life, the pertinent personal question is: How do we *apply* the energy we consume? How should we apply our energy?

Focus

As a child you may have experimented with a magnifying glass in the sunshine. By focusing the sun's rays you could set paper alight. In the technological world, laser focus brought us microchips that helped produce this book. If you ask anyone about their success, focus will likely have been a key feature.

Our brains are not wired to be good at multitasking non-routine activities. We might feel good when we are busily multitasking, but we are not necessarily productive. While distraction can keep us sane at times, especially around mundane activities, when it comes to difficult tasks then distraction is the enemy of effort. Do one thing at a time. Give it your full attention. Author Gary Keller reminds us that:

"Until my ONE thing is done, everything else is a distraction". Focus is simply another example of the controlled application of energy. It is very powerful. When there is something important to do, eliminate all other distractions and do it. You may need to reconsider your environment. Does it have many distractions? If so, you need to rethink your work set-up. How you schedule your activities during a typical day is also important. There are times in the day when we are naturally more productive, and we should schedule our more demanding tasks to coincide. Our energy is finite, so we can't be in full focus all the time. Nutrition and rest are critical.

Moving From Reaction to Enthusiasm

Beyond focus, how can we make more productive use of personal energy?

To answer this we can think about energy in three ascending levels. The base level of energy application is where we are *reactive*. Something happens and we react. At this level we sit back and observe what the world throws at us, habitually or subconsciously reacting with no motivation other than to react. There is nothing wrong with this, but perhaps there is more to life than responding to emails, text messages and tweets. All too often we delegate our destiny to the random rivers of chance. In this mode our energy use is reactive or sometimes defensive.

A more productive, higher energy level is when we become *proactive*. Now this has a more deliberate feel to it. We choose to do something on *our* initiative – starting new conversations for example, or coming up with better questions. Virtually all progress depends upon proactivity.

But we can do even better and go one step further.

Our most productive state is when we are *enthusiastic*. This combines being proactive with a real sense of purpose. Enthusiasm is infectious in a good way. At the time of writing, a Google search for synonyms of enthusiasm returns some of the following results: eagerness, keenness, ardour, fervour, *warmth*, passion, zeal, zest, vivacity, *energy*, verve, vigour, dynamism, *fire* and spirit. Enthusiasm is a wonderful trait. You can *feel* it. We find enthusiasm at the intersection of energy and purpose. For enthusiasm to endure, the purpose needs to be principled, that is, be grounded in wholesome motivations.

Proceeding with enthusiasm is both a pleasant and a productive route to developing skills. Enthusiasm becomes the lightning rod for learning. Doing things because you *want* to, not because you feel you *have* to.

Enthusiasm doesn't have to be loud. Quiet enthusiasm is effective and sustainable. A glint in the eye is clear to all. You will know this already if you have spent time with someone who is enthusiastic. Notice how enthusiastic people enhance your energy, while others can sap it.

Discover what enthuses you and discover the power of positive energy. Be an energy magnifier. Choose enthusiasm.

Chapter Seventeen:
Experiences

> *The purpose of life is to live it, to taste experience to the utmost, to reach out eagerly and without fear for newer and richer experience.*
>
> - Eleanor Roosevelt

D o you prefer things or experiences? Consider the following scenario. It is late autumn and you are home alone, settling in with a good book in front of a log fire that you have diligently brought to a nice crackle. You head to the kitchen to brew a cup of coffee, only to return to a fire that is out of control caused by a spark from one of the logs. You run back to the kitchen to grab some water, or anything to help quench the flames, but quickly realise that it is too dangerous to stay in the house and you have to get out – and get out quickly. Without thinking, you give yourself a split second to save something from the flames before you scramble to safety.

What do you save?

If you are like many people, photographs or personal diaries are often the instinctive choice. Why is it that when faced with the choice of saving *one* thing we don't save the most expensive thing? In fact, a photograph is more than just a physical object, it is a representation of a memory, a past experience. A marking of time, once there, now gone.

You see, the best things in life are not things. They are experiences. What we truly treasure springs from experiences.

Experiences Trump Things

As a large portion of the world's population moves above the subsistence level, engaging experiences are trumping things in the pursuit of happiness. We are entering an era where engaging experiences are what light our emotional fire.

As you think about what to do with your precious spare time and hard-earned cash, carefully consider the choice between material goods and engaging experiences. People tend to derive more lasting happiness from experiences. Happiness from things is transitory, but the joy from experiences is enduring.

Experiences are the essence of enjoyment or sometimes pain, depending on the situation. They are always at the root of wisdom. This may be one area where it is harder to put wise heads on young shoulders. It takes time to have a diverse range of experiences. Certain experiences simply can't be rushed or accelerated. The laws of nature apply. But we can give ourselves a head start by seeking out a diversity of experiences early in life and by savouring and reflecting on those experiences. We often don't give enough time to reflecting on our experiences. It is worth asking ourselves questions like: What happened here? Why did I enjoy it? Why did I hate it? What did I learn about myself? What will I think about differently going forward? What will I do differently in future?

If you want to understand something, experience it. I could describe the smell of coffee to you, but if you have never actually experienced it, it doesn't matter how technical my explanation or how sophisticated your understanding is, you will not fully understand it. There is simply no substitute for experience. The same goes for sex, which is one of the few experiences that combine all the senses of taste, touch, smell, sight and sound. Elaborate explanation is no substitute for the real thing.

What have been some of the best experiences you have had to date? Why those experiences? For many people the most memorable experiences are ones that *changed* them in some way. They helped them grow. Travel is a great way to experience different cultures and to enrich our perspectives. Time spent doing interesting things with friends is one of the most fruitful experiences of all.

In the pursuit of experiences, we can seek to be entertained or we can get involved. By getting involved we dare to do. And there is no substitute for doing. Someone once bought me a white T-shirt embossed with the words DON'T TELL ME, SHOW ME. This was a call to action.

Knowledge Versus Experience

The advent of smartphones is giving billions of people instantaneous access to facts – a mini brain in our pocket. Facts are easily found. Having a head full of facts is no longer a differentiator when facts have become commoditised. Recall Richard Feynman's comments on the distinction between knowing what something is called and understanding it.

What does it mean to say someone is very experienced? It is usually a compliment. But what if the experience comes from doing something highly specialised – like the person who has dedicated their entire life to understanding the molecular structure of egg shells? Or the world's most accomplished plate spinner?

Experience can be narrow or wide. Everyone will have their own preference. If you want to have interesting stories to tell your grandchildren, wide may be the way to go. If we have an open mind to new experiences we can treat lots of decisions as experiments. How they work out is not as important as the intrinsic value of the new experience.

Experiential choice has just gone exponential. The web has opened multiple doors to a wide range of choices that once would have been considered in the realm of science fiction. At its core the web has created a whole new world of virtual experiences. But even more importantly we can use the reach of the web to seek out other people with similar interests to us irrespective of how varied or specialised our preferences are.

We won't be able to experience everything and that's perfectly okay. Absence of experience can occasionally be useful. For example, experience absence is a very reasonable excuse for not "knowing". The next time you are asked for your opinion on a difficult topic, where you might otherwise feel embarrassed not to have an opinion, simply respond: "I am not the right person to answer, as I don't have any *direct experience* in that area." The subtext is that any self-appointed "experts" better have real experience if they are to be credible. Opinions are interesting but experience really counts.

Facts fill the mind; experiences open it. When you get the opportunity to experience something different, take it. Differentiate yourself through your diversity of experiences.

Chapter Eighteen:
Where to Live

> *Without question both of those decisions – the what and the who – mean a great deal to our lives. But there is another decision that has an equal, if not greater effect on our economic future, happiness, and overall life outcome: the 'where factor'.*
>
> - Richard Florida
> Extract from *Who's Your City?*

Three questions: Where would you love to live? Why that place? If you are not living there now, why not?

Freedom of movement, and the economic capacity to move, are improving all the time. Our choices are far more diverse than those of our ancestors. Where to live is also a very personal choice. The wide diversity of people and the places in which they reside are testament to the personality of place.

Notwithstanding our free will and the many

possibilities, might the place we live be determined more by chance than by choice? Where we are born, study or first find work are all significant residential anchors. Where we live may be incidental to where we or our partner works or grew up, or where our parents live, a context that significantly narrows the radius of choice. In fact, very few people begin by finding a great place to live, around which they then build the rest of their lives. Usually we just end up somewhere as a by-product of other choices or circumstances.

I have divided the exploration of where to live into three categories: logical, personal and emotional.

Logical Considerations. The following characteristics are probably desirable to most people in choosing a place to live. If you are already living somewhere that has these attributes, count yourself very lucky. Things many of us take for granted are but a pipe dream for others. Logical considerations include:

- Comprehensive and accessible social infrastructure (public transport, education, personal safety, and healthcare).
- Ample and varied employment opportunities.
- A stable rule of law that protects individual rights.

Good availability of work is critical, especially as we now change careers more often. A trend towards urbanisation is clustering employment opportunities in larger urban centres. While technological connectivity increases the availability of more varied careers from remote places, physical clustering of like-minded people still drives employment opportunity.

Personal Considerations. There is the age-old question of whether we would rather be a big fish in a small pond or a small fish in a big pond. Personal considerations include whether we prefer cities over towns, urban over rural, warm climates over cold, or one type of political system over another. We may live somewhere that is not perfect for our current needs but will be later, and we are happy to be patient and choose to delay gratification. Our personal considerations change over time. People with young families will have different preferences to retirees. Migration to warmer climates in old age can help with some illnesses and there is evidence of the health benefits of living near the coast. Don't, however, expect a change of climate, in itself, to increase your happiness. Though we may think that moving to a sunny place will lift our spirits, we quickly adapt to our new environment. The same goes for living in a larger house. Again we quickly adapt to our new surroundings. What matters is not the house in which we live but the home that we make.

Emotional Considerations. Emotional considerations are governed more by who we live with than where we live. The who is not just in our home but also in our neighbourhood, town or city. Feeling that we fit within our community of people matters to our sense of place and purpose. The desire to belong is a deeply rooted one. There is no substitute for trusted and kind neighbours, close friends and being among people who are generally optimistic. I have lived in Ireland and in Australia. Sydney is a great city. Yet some of the enjoyment was dampened by not being able to share experiences with distant friends. For many of us, I suspect that who we live with is at least if not more important than where we live. We may rationalise working away from our families for better financial security, but we should also consider the emotional benefits of being with our loved ones.

A Thought on Citizenship. Many countries allow people to apply for citizenship without having to give up the citizenship of their country of origin. Often this right extends to future children. If you are working away from your home country it makes a lot of sense to stay long enough to apply for citizenship. This will give both you and your possible future children a broader array of choices later on. Even if you never use it, the option to pack up and try a new experience is worth having.

Where we live too often comes down to chance, as a by-product of other decisions or as a compromise. Recognising that where we live is an important life choice should cause us to give the decision more thought.

Chapter Nineteen:
The One for Me

So that is marriage, Lily thought, a man and
a woman looking at a girl throwing a ball.
                 - Virginia Woolf

If you are already married you might want to skip this and go directly to the next chapter.

She is the one for him. He is the one for her. They were childhood sweethearts who knew they were right for each other and after twenty years they are still blissfully married. You may know some couples who match this description. The perfect match.

Is there someone out there who is just right for us, and how do we find them?

Before we answer that question, consider the following. Assume you live in a society where arranged marriages are the custom. As the chief of the society you get to make the matches. The rules are that the couples must stay together for at least three years. After three years they can choose to part company or to stay together. You have been doing this for a long time and have earned a deserved reputation for making great matches. In fact, your record is outstanding. There have only been a small number of couples who decided to go their own way when the three years were up.

What factors do you think might explain this matchmaking success? Realistic expectations and personal compatibility may figure strongly.

Now let's consider whether there is a better question. If you wanted to increase the likelihood of proposed couples *breaking up*, what kinds of matches would you make?

Think of some people you know who have grown apart. Were there factors at play that made breakup likely? An added nuance is whether the breakup was the fault of one person, both persons, or indeed neither person.

Let's assume that you are the one who is being matched up. You can choose the attributes that you don't want to see in the person being picked for you. What would they be? What would you not like to see in a prospective partner?

Accepting that individual preferences vary widely, I suspect many of us may want to think twice when we see too many of the following characteristics:

- Anyone with unrealistic expectations!
- Someone with no close friends.
- Someone with no sense of humour.
- Those with an overly pessimistic orientation.
- Anyone we want to change, think we can change or who wants to change us.
- Someone who does not speak our language, literally or figuratively.

- Those who are bad-tempered, mean, domineering or incapable of change.
- Someone we have just met and have not had a chance to get to know.
- Someone we feel we can't have good conversations with now, or in ten years' time.
- Someone who is *widely* different in age, maturity, culture or belief systems.

The question of whether we marry, and if so whom, is a serious one. In terms of happiness in life it is one of the most important decisions that we will ever make, yet we learn little about choosing a partner through our formal education. There are plenty of clichés like "Love is blind and marriage is an eye opener". Though Ben Franklin was more thoughtful when he advised, "Keep your eyes open before marriage, and half shut afterwards."

When we consider the importance of the decision, there is surprisingly little serious guidance. Much of our guidance comes from observing our parents. And that is a lottery, a single case study. It probably does give us some sensitivities around what to avoid. Yet it conditions our views on what to expect.

Expectations matter greatly. I believe we should have high hopes and low expectations. The success rate of arranged marriages has a lot to do with expectations. Expectations were realistic. This doesn't mean that you should settle for second best.

What is the essence of marriage? Two quotes from the German philosopher Nietzsche are relevant: "It is not a lack of love, but a lack of friendship that makes unhappy marriages"; and "When entering into a marriage one ought to ask oneself: do you believe you are going to enjoy talking with this woman up into your old age? Everything else in marriage is transitory, but most of the time you are together will be devoted to conversation." Nietzsche sees marriage as a special class of friendship. Marriage is a friendship that is best grounded in mutual respect and a contentment with being in each other's company.

So, when it comes to the question of whom to marry, perhaps we could rephrase the question as who would be a great long-term friend.

There is also a wonderful related passage in Gibran's *The Prophet* which goes as follows:

Sing and dance together and be joyous, but let each of you be alone,
Even as the strings of a lute are alone though they quiver with the same music.

The power of attraction has a resonance to it.

Knowing what you want is a good start. Getting what you want is quite another matter. To this point I like Charlie Munger's advice: "What's the best way to get a good spouse? The best single way is to deserve a good spouse because a good spouse is by definition not nuts."

Who is the one for me? If we think of marriage as a special form of friendship, then, prospectively at least, the idea of there being *one* person who is right for us doesn't ring true. After the fact is arguably a slightly different matter. We have the psychological impact of what's been termed the "endowment effect" at play (whereby things that are ours suddenly seem more valuable), and any beliefs, rational or otherwise, that strengthen a friendship are good. A more appropriate characterisation may be that my partner is *the one I have chosen*. As marriage is a huge commitment, it would be satisfying to know that we have chosen wisely.

When it comes to choice of partner, a new dynamic is in play. The advent of online matchmaking has expanded the field of potentially compatible candidates. Only time will tell, but I suspect that the science of online matchmaking may open up new possibilities. Less reliance on the serendipity of a chance encounter. A window perhaps to be more proactive than reactive. Enthusiastic even. Just watch out for the paradox of choice (too much choice can be overwhelming and prevent action) and for the risk of wandering into uncharted waters. There is a reason childhood sweethearts from small towns make good marriage partners. They are already good friends and likely had reasonable and similar expectations.

Another way to explore the question of 'who to marry' is to look at the causes of breakups. Dr John Gottman has dedicated his entire career to studying marital stability and divorce prediction. By simply observing a couple in conversation he has developed an uncanny ability to predict whether the relationship will last. My wife and I won't be inviting John to dinner anytime soon. Gottman's methodology is to identify the balance between positive and negative emotional cues. Too much negativity, and a relationship is heading for the rocks. Defensiveness, stonewalling, criticism and contempt are particularly corrosive. Stonewalling is the worst of all. Watch for these characteristics in your potential partner and in yourself.

Know yourself, be yourself, mind yourself – these are also extremely important here. Often we choose partners that we feel can fix us or vice versa. This leads to trouble. You can fix or change nobody but yourself. If we choose a partner based on fixing or filling what is lacking in ourselves it can create a power struggle within the relationship, which is never a good way to start a marriage. Fix yourself first!

Another important factor when choosing a partner is to ensure you both share a similar moral code. When it comes to difficulties later on in the relationship – and there will be some – a common moral code will help in deciding the best way forward. When the code is in sync it is easier to come to a fair understanding that will please both parties.

Two parting comments. Firstly, I don't have anything useful to say on the topic of whether one should marry. I will leave this to Socrates: "By all means, marry. If you get a good wife, you'll become happy; if you get a bad one, you'll become a philosopher." Secondly, when you find the right person don't mess it up. You may not get a second chance.

The Four Pillars of finding a good marriage partner:

Pillar One: *Take your time. Whom to marry is probably the most important decision you will ever make.*

Pillar Two: *Don't settle. Be aware of the most obvious warning signals and don't expect to change your partner (or you will most likely end up changing partners).*

Pillar Three: *Look for long-term friendship that is grounded in mutual respect and enjoyment of each other's company.*

Pillar Four: *Deserve a good partner.*

Chapter Twenty:
Having Children

Writing books is the closest men ever come to childbearing.

- Norman Mailer

If you have ever been on an aeroplane and been close to a whinging boy, your reaction will likely depend on whether you have children yourself. The childless among us will be wondering why the obviously incompetent parents can't get the annoying critter to shut up. The parents among us will be just happy that he's not our child.

Whether to have children is certainly one of our most important life choices. For many the choice of whether to have children is easy. Either they are in the majority who have a natural urge to procreate, or they are at the other end of the spectrum and don't see what all the fuss is about. Everyone has his or her own motivations based on life experiences and expectations. Unfortunately for many there is no choice. While adoption or fostering may be an option for some, there are far too many people who don't get a chance to have children of their own.

The Family Choice

What if you don't have a strong desire either way? What should guide your decision?

Unfortunately this is one of the few areas where there is no realistic trial run, and vicarious learning is not an option either. Having children is an "all-in" endeavour. It is unusual in this respect. Parents and childless adults alike simply can't fully appreciate the *relative* merits of their respective situations. They can only know one state, and any judgements on relative merits are by definition incomplete.

We can't appreciate in advance that raising children requires so much hard work. The responsibility that accompanies raising children is a heavy one. For a long while our children are totally dependent on us. Despite the importance of the decision, we receive little if any preparation and no practical way of understanding the degree of personal sacrifice. Little thought, little preparation and no training. Hardly a recipe for success.

Having children:

- tests our patience, our endurance, and, after consecutive sleepless nights, our very sanity
- recasts, and often severely strains, our other relationships, in particular our relationship with our partner
- puts us under financial pressure and can thereby hold us in jobs we dislike
- widens our range of emotional experiences from the highs to the lows

- severely curtails spontaneity
- heightens our senses so that we instinctively smell, see or hear danger, even when it's not serious.

You may then ask why we voluntarily put ourselves through such a decades-long marathon. The biological urge to procreate is so strong that the 'choice' is not completely voluntary. And indeed it is sometimes accidental. As the saying goes, before having children I had three theories on the subject, now I have three children and no theories. As a father I can only relay my own experience thus far. To cut to the chase: despite all the sacrifices I wouldn't have it any other way. Now you can argue that I would say that, given our psychological bias to love what's ours. But it goes beyond that. Some of the most deeply satisfying moments of my life have been experiencing our children:

- having fun together
- doing things for each other
- joyfully lost in an engaging activity
- laughing or singing
- showing natural love and affection
- developing their own distinct personalities and capabilities.

And there is much more. Through our children we can get a strong sense of purpose and focus. The loving bond between parent and child is one of the strongest there is. This is why the loss of a child is possibly the greatest loss of all. We would do anything to protect our children, although I use the word "our" guardedly. In truth children are their own unique persons and in no way belong to us, in the "ownership" sense of the word. They may be in our custody, but they are never in our control. The time will come for our children to leave the nest. It can be heart-wrenching to see them go, but go they must. Writer and poet Khalil Gibran put it well:

> *Your children are not your children*
> *They are sons and daughters of life's*
> *longing for itself.*

For most people the decision on whether to have children will come naturally to them. Nature does its thing. We should however be mindful of our motivations. We may want to think twice if we are having children to "lock in" a partner, add another achievement to the list, mind us in our old age, or simply follow what we see most others do. The ticking biological clock is another powerful motivator, with the fear of regret sometimes driving the decision (though the possibility to freeze eggs may provide relief in some cases).

Before having children we should consider whether we are emotionally mature enough to make, and follow through with, such a consequential decision. Are we up to the challenge? To treat our children well we need to know and respect ourselves.

Just as important as the choice to have children, is the choice of who will be there by our side. We need all the support we can get. Single parenthood is especially difficult, but perhaps not as hard as parenthood by feuding partners. Having wider family support available to parents is a real blessing. Kind grandparents can be wonderful role models for children, a source of non-judgemental encouragement.

Dispelling Some Myths

We are at our happiest when we are bringing up children. "In the moment" studies of happiness have shown that the opposite is frequently true. Our happier times seem to be before and after kids. We remember our time with children more favourably than our actual experience at the time.

It is selfish not to have children. Society can be intolerant of those who choose to be childfree. Voluntary childlessness is frowned upon. Society is jealous of the "dinky" double-income no-kids professional couple with their exotic annual holidays. Deriding childfree couples is hypocritical. We celebrate free choice in almost every other sphere, and we should be willing to do so when someone decides that there is more to life than Darwinian procreation. Indeed, many childless teachers, politicians, community and religious workers have dedicated their time to serving broader society, and done so with a passion and fervour that might not have been possible if they had had children of their own.

We will always be great parents. Yes, we all think that we can be perfect, but we have our moments. The loud angry parent shouting at their teenage son, well, that's most of us in our weaker moments.

Babies sleep more soundly when the baby monitor is turned off. Fathers do.

Parenting

What then is our goal as parents?

Two important things are: (i) showing uncondi-tional love, and (ii) fostering our children's self-esteem. The goal is that our children know they are loved and know they are capable.

If we can release young adults that have inner confidence in their unique capacity to live life fully, we should be able to reflect with pride as they go on to be positive and productive members of society. With this parenting privilege, we will have loved and we will have left a legacy.

Having and raising children is not a fair-weather pursuit, yet those who have them wouldn't have it any other way. Our ability to fully control whether we have children is open to debate, but the choice to love them, no strings attached, is ours alone.

Chapter Twenty-One:
Compound Gratification

Money is of a prolific generating nature.
Money can beget Money and its Offspring can
beget more.

- Benjamin Franklin

There are some questions that are not asked in polite company or indeed among friends. How much money you have or earn is one such question.

Everyone's relationship to money is different and our attitudes are shaped by our upbringing and life experiences. The old saying goes that money can't buy happiness, but it sure as hell buys a better class of misery. Our sensitivity to asking, or being asked, about money has a lot to do with the wide and contradictory meanings we attribute to money. Do we have money or does money have us? Is money a security blanket or a wet blanket?

In Chapter Eight we explored how comparison breeds fear. Money invites crude comparisons. We don't hear about the "poor and famous".

Of course money is meaningless if there is no

future, and having money provides no guarantee of contentment or safety. The degree to which we accumulate money reflects many things including a judgement call on our mortality coupled with an illusion of control.

Yet for all its evils I suspect most of us would rather have some than not, and it is against that backdrop that we look at the nature of long-term saving. When we save we make the choice to forgo current consumption with a view to consumption at a later time. We defer gratification. Our discussion covers three areas:

1. The psychology of saving
2. The mathematics of saving
3. A framework for saving.

The Psychology of Saving

An early capacity to delay gratification is predictive of future social and cognitive competence. When an animal is presented with food it will usually eat it. This is the natural thing to do. There are psychological reasons why we are not entirely rational when it comes to saving for the distant future. One is our inability to intelligently imagine our future selves. It is difficult to envisage the value to us of the savings in ten or twenty years' time. We struggle to put our arm around what we will feel like in the future, so the benefits of a large future savings pot are not real or tangible to us.

Another factor is our inability to weigh or "discount" the distant future. People regularly, and lower animals always, favour smaller sooner over larger later. Indeed, beyond a certain point we place minimal value on even substantial sums of money if we can't get our hands on it for a very long time. Our behaviour is known as "hyperbolic discounting" and it helps explain why we are generally poor at saving for retirement. We overvalue the present and under-value the far future. There is some logic to this, as we may not survive to see the distant future.

The Mathematics of Saving

Albert Einstein said, "compound interest is the eighth wonder of the world. He who understands it, earns it...He who doesn't...pays it."

The power of compounding is extraordinary. Understanding its value goes to the core of successful saving. Assume you set aside $10,000 and it is invest-ed for twenty years. If you earned 4% per annum compounded then you would have over $20,000 at the end. If the annual compound rate of return was 12% your final sum would be close to $100,000.

Avoiding mistakes is also crucial to wealth pres-ervation. The mathematics of mistakes is miserable. The two most common sources of mistakes are: (i) not knowing what you are doing; and (ii) leverage (i.e. borrowing or debt). At times leverage can be appropri-ate (e.g. an affordable level to purchase your home); however, more people have gone broke through excess borrowing than in any other way. Be extremely wary of it. On borrowing, Warren Buffet advised that if you are smart you don't need it and if you are not you have no business using it.

Chapter Twenty-One

A Framework for Saving

Here we introduce four cornerstones of sensible saving.

Cornerstone One: Maximise your capacity to save. This is about spending less than we earn. Simple as it sounds, our expenditure has a nasty habit of increasing to match, or worse exceed, our earnings. To maximise our savings capacity we need to spend less, earn more, or both.

You may feel that your current circumstances don't allow you to save. What if you experienced a 5% pay cut? The likelihood is that your expenses would reduce out of necessity. If you are not currently saving, give yourself a 5% pay cut and set that aside for the future.

Cornerstone Two: Commit to a regular and automatic savings plan. Decide that you will save a fixed amount of your monthly earnings from now on. It could be somewhere between 5% and 20%. Resolve not to reduce it. Let your friends know that this is a principle of yours – something that you have made a very conscious decision to do. Make the saving automatic. It could be a payroll deduction at source or an automatic monthly transfer from your checking account to an investment account.

To help with your resolve, think again about the mathematics of compounding. I named this chapter compound gratification rather than the more commonly used deferred gratification, as the latter understates the true value of sensible long-term saving. You see, saving has another benefit beyond the compounding savings pool. It is the positive mental

160

feedback loop of demonstrated self-control, much in the same way as sticking to a good diet or exercise regime. Think also about the wider number of personal choices that will be available to you in later life if you have saved well. If you have saved and invested rationally, benefits are deferred – but crucially they are also compounded.

Cornerstone Three: Invest rationally. Rational in this context means being coldly logical. Much has been written on the topic of investment. Some of the best investment writers I have come across are referenced in *Appendix I – Still Curious?* Two points are worth understanding at the outset:

- Rational investing is a difficult discipline that few have mastered.
- Much of the investment, savings and related financial advisory industry is more concerned with their economics than with yours. (A good read on this topic is Fred Schwed's *Where are the Customers' Yachts?*).

That said, the question then is where do we start? Remember again that we are talking about long-term investing here. Warren Buffett, one of the world's most successful investors, recently said that when he dies he has asked the executors of his will to put 90% of his wealth in a low-cost index tracker that tracks the S&P 500 (an equity index of leading large companies) and 10% in a low-cost short-dated government bond fund. The 10% liquid bond allocation is to allow for unforeseen expenses, averting the need to sell the S&P 500 index tracker in an emergency. Buffett's advice is targeted at the vast majority of people who are not investment professionals and don't have the inclination for DIY investing. The advice is very rational. It is grounded on the stark reality that the majority of investment professionals (for all their qualifications and experience) underperform a low-cost S&P 500 index.

If you have a genuine interest in investing then spending the time to manage your own investments is intellectually rewarding, and if you are good enough (few are), it is financially rewarding. The DIY approach is beyond the scope of this book. Good books to start with are David Swensen's *Unconventional Success* or Joel Greenblatt's *You Can Be a Stock Market Genius*.

In addition to the passive or DIY choices, we have a third choice: to have our savings managed by a trusted investment manager. The difficulty here is in choosing wisely. Most people hire and fire investment managers at precisely the wrong time. Managers are too often fired after poor periods and hired after good ones. The tendency for returns to average out over time means that it can be more rational to do the opposite. Few people have the fortitude to lean against the wind. While choosing a good investment manager is difficult, the rewards are substantial. Small differences in performance generate huge variances when compounded over long periods. If you go down the route of choosing a trusted investment manager, I suggest the following approach:

- Split your savings pool across a few managers whom you feel you can trust and who have most of their own personal net worth invested in the same vehicle that you are considering.

- Ensure that each manager has a minimum ten year track record of strong results, preferably spanning a full business cycle.

- Pick managers with different investment styles, that is, managers who have generated their returns in different ways.

- Only hire managers who can clearly explain their philosophy, are passionate about their craft, and are honest in their reporting to investors. While good IQ is important – exceptional EQ is essential.

- If you don't feel confident in picking a good manager, get professional help with your decision (I hear your objection that if you can't pick a manager, how could you pick an advisor – but surely there is someone who can help.)

Cornerstone Four: Minimise costs. Buffet's instructions for his inheritance go to the corrosive impact of expenses. Expenses are not just confined to annual management and administration fees. They also include transaction fees. All expenses are bad for your financial health. Much of the advisory and brokerage community is incentivised to "churn" portfolios, which generates more trading commissions.

Tax can be a large cost that eats into returns. Tax efficiency is a crucial component in building long-term wealth. Get professional advice here. Look in particular at whether you are fully utilising the tax-free compounding capacity of pension or retirement plans for both you and, if married, your spouse. Many jurisdictions have especially favourable regimes to encourage saving for retirement.

The third cost is inflation, in that it eats into your real purchasing power. That cost can't be reduced; you need to rely on investment performance outpacing inflation.

Earn more. Spend less. Set up a regular savings plan and make a public commitment to maintain it. Make savings automatic. Invest rationally through a passive, DIY, or trusted manager route. Avoid large mistakes. Do your homework and be careful of leverage. Minimise expenses. Maximise tax efficiency. Think about the compound gratification of knowing that you have chosen the smart route – enriching the choices you will have later in life. Done properly, the longer-term enrichment of choice created by a rational savings plan is a multiple of the current sacrifice. If saving is automatic it may not even feel like a sacrifice. Choose larger later over smaller sooner.

Chapter Twenty-Two:
Thinking

Don't think twice, it's alright.

- Bob Dylan

We would like to believe that we have good control over our thoughts, reactions and decision-making processes, but the truth is that we are subject to biases and unconscious influences that hijack our capacity to make good choices. This chapter explores how our brains work, why we make errors and what we can do about it. We also consider the nature of creativity.

The Mental Mound

Let's start with an analogy. Think of our brain as being like a mound of clay. When we are born the clay is soft and malleable. It has high plasticity and is quite amenable to change. Learning experiences have the effect of squirting water from a syringe onto the mental mound. The water forms patterns or streams. These become self-reinforcing. New water is more likely to follow previous patterns. These patterns define the topology of the mound. They are creating a type of neural navigation network. When we need to navigate the mound, we are well served if there is a rich tapestry of routes available to us. Different experiences build new routes.

As we age the mental mound of clay becomes less malleable but thankfully remains ever capable of changing. Even if it becomes rock hard, we can chisel away at it. All experiences, thoughts and perceptions are continually working on the navigation system. For example, if we spend a lot of time watching mindless reality TV, our brains are undergoing continuous micro-surgeries and yet we rarely consider what this is doing to our neural navigation network.

We can think of the network as consisting of highways and byways. For lots of routine actions we can happily wander down the highway without think-ing twice. This is crucial. Functions like walking occur without conscious thought. As we get dressed in the morning, we don't want to spend too much time wondering whether we should put on our left shoe or our right shoe first. We rightly don't spend too much time thinking about the vast majority of routine activ-ities. If we did, life would become intolerably slow.

There are other more important activities which are better served by taking a different route, a side-road. Navigating the byways is more purposeful and demanding. This is why we make poor decisions when tired or hungry. For important decisions the advice to "sleep on it" is wise indeed.

Problems arise from having a limited navigation network or from freewheeling down a highway when we should be trekking through a byway.

Mental Muggings

Though we are supposed to be rational we are prone to all sorts of biases. Charlie Munger did a great job of summarising these in a lecture entitled *The Psychology of Human Misjudgement*. Daniel Kahneman also comprehensively tackled the topic with *Thinking Fast and Slow*. We routinely make illogical decisions. Advances in neuroscience help us understand why, but unfortunately even when we understand them we are better at seeing the flaws in *others* than we are at seeing them in *ourselves*. Some of the more interesting "mental muggings" are as follows:

Dog with a bone (loss aversion). We hate losing things. Typically we weigh losses twice as heavily as we value gains. This causes us to react very negatively if someone tries to take something from us. It also helps explain why we are reluctant to cut our losses, preferring instead to keep going in the vain hope that we may break even.

Interests not reasons (the incentive bias). When seeking to persuade, appeal to interests not reason. As we learned in Chapter Four, the power of incentives is pervasive.

Your fault, not mine (the "fundamental attribution" effect). There is a difference in the way we see the actions of others and our own actions. When others do things, we see their behaviour as a representation of their true nature rather than a reaction to our behaviour. So when someone else is hostile, we see it as part of their innate personality. When we are hostile we see it as a reaction to their hostility. We see what we do as a reaction to circumstances rather than as a problem with our nature.

I'm on top of this (the illusion of control). We over-estimate what is in our control and underestimate the role of chance. Entrepreneurs overestimate their chances of success. This is good for society because if entrepreneurs were totally rational they might not try to develop new products and services. In business affairs, the illusion of control also results in competitor neglect. We focus disproportionately on what we think we can do and not enough on what our competitors are doing.

The glove fits (the coherent story bias). This is perhaps the most pervasive bias of all. Our lives are fundamentally about "me and my story". We are constantly rewriting the story in our heads, and very often our recollection (what Kahneman calls our *remembering selves*) is different to what really happened (our *experiencing selves*). Though illogical, this is not necessarily always a bad thing. To the extent that we can have a good story about ourselves, we can face the world with an optimistic resilience.

The problem with stories is that they incorrectly weigh consistency over completeness and surprise over significance.

You may also have noticed how we love to invent reasons for things, frequently mistaking correlation for causation.

If someone gives us a reason for something, we are inclined to accept it, even if the merits are suspect. Munger calls it our *reason-respecting tendency*. The next time you want to skip a queue at an airport, go to the top of the line and say "I am under time pressure to catch a plane". You will be surprised how many people accept your "reason".

I have it handy (the availability bias). Kahneman calls this "what you see is all there is". We ascribe greater weight to more recent facts, more vivid facts or the story that seems most coherent. We tend to accept our first conclusions.

Highlights and happy endings. They were onto something at the wedding of Cana when they saved the best wine till last. Apart from peaks and troughs, we also disproportionately remember and value endings. My sister trained in a high-end London hair salon and learned to make the last five minutes of every customer's encounter special. By contrast, if you have ever sat through a movie with a poor ending, you will understand how a bad ending can ruin an otherwise good story.

The ABC of Creativity

There is a view that creativity is innate and cannot be learned or developed. We are either creative or not – like pregnancy, there is no in-between. This black-or-white view is partly explained by the limits of language. The word *creativity* can have different meanings. It is context dependent. Think of there being two types of creativity. "A-tivity" represents aesthetic creativity:

art, design, music, film. "B-tivity" represents benefit creativity. This opens up a much more familiar world in which we all have contributions to make. With B-tivity we may think of anything we can do to improve things in either our work or personal lives. Any action that improves on something else demonstrates B-tivity. We are all capable of B-tivity.

If we understand the workings of the brain, we can develop tools to facilitate creativity, which, to stick with our theme for this chapter, is about finding new routes. Say you are out driving when your car breaks down. It is towed to a nearby garage and you get a taxi home. On the journey home you may discover a route that you had not seen before. This happens because you were literally taken to another place. Thinking guru Edward de Bono has done great work on the practical tools to force our brains down different tracks to assist with creativity. The tools are very effective because they are *not* natural. One such tool is provocation. In the world of chemistry provocation is used to force compounds to work in different ways. The same principle can be used with thinking. Say for example I was to suggest (i.e., provoke) the idea that new employees should pay their employers instead of the other way round. While this may sound foolish at first, once you start to work with that constraint your brain starts thinking in more creative ways. For example, the employers may offer one of the best on-the-job training programmes in the world, a practical university if you will.

Humour also offers clues to understanding how our brains work, and can be an excellent source of creativity. The whole premise of humour is to take us on a different track. Dreams can do this also. I once had a dream that I was Chinese. When I woke up, I was disoriented. If you are a kleptomaniac you probably didn't get it. It's hard to explain puns to kleptomaniacs because they're always taking things literally. Humour takes us off the highway. One of my favourites is from Groucho Marx: "A child of five would understand this. Send someone to fetch a child of five."

Our brains are powerful but far from perfect. While our gut, intuition and subconscious serve us well, for important decisions we need to think twice. Understanding how our brains operate improves our ability to use them.

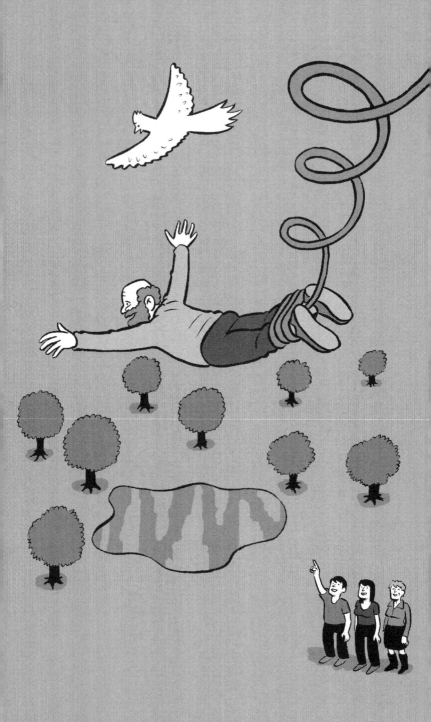

Chapter Twenty-Three:
Full Circle

To Contemplation's sober eye
Such is the race of man:
And they that creep, and they that fly,
Shall end where they began.

- Thomas Gray,
from *Ode on the Spring,* written in 1748

The above quote was given to me by my father-in-law. He heard it from his father. There were smarter people around long before us. And they will be here long after we are gone.

Life has many chapters – an endless unfolding. I hope you enjoyed reading this book, and that you stopped along the way. I certainly enjoyed writing it. We covered a lot of ground together, from what we do to who we are, from whom to marry to where we live, from what motivates to what matters, and lots in between. Thanks for taking the journey with me. It was an ambitious expedition, all the time guided by wiser heads than mine.

While our theme has been the search to put wise heads on young shoulders, there also comes a time when we might put young shoulders under wise heads. Our later years can be sprinkled with youthful enthusiasm.

Canadian zoologist and writer N.J. Berrill put it elegantly:

> *Our problem now is to remain human in spite of growing older, to keep the keen edge of living and to fuse the intelligence and the heart of youth with the wisdom that comes with time.*

Psychologist Erik Erikson categorised life's stages. In the last stage, which he kindly calls late adulthood, Erikson outlines how we spend much of our time reflecting on the life we have lived. If we have lived life with a sense of fulfilment, we can face aging, and ultimately death, with a feeling of integrity.

When we get to the very end, what might our epitaphs say? We all have our own take – that's what makes life interesting. Here is a sample from some of my friends:

> *"She knew what mattered most"*
>
> *"There is never a wrong time to do the right thing"*
>
> *"Always be there for your family and never give up"*
>
> *"A great friend, a kind heart and a passionate learner"*
>
> *"Did more good than harm and had fun doing it"*
>
> *"Loved by his family, respected by all"*
>
> *"Drew from life as much as possible"*
>
> *"A good husband, a good father, a good son and a good friend"*
>
> *"Leave the dead to bury the dead"*
>
> *"He did his best"*

*"Energy cannot be created or destroyed, it can only
    be changed from one form to another"*

"Life was great, I have no regrets"

*"Like a bird on a wire, like a drunk in a midnight
    choir, I have lived my life to be free"*

".....and now for some answers"

As I thought about what my single line summary
might be, I changed my mind a few times but
eventually settled on:

"He was good to be around"

Einstein said that life is like riding a bicycle. To keep
your balance, you must keep moving. We started out
with endless curiosity. Why not end as we began?

Pebbles of Perception

The pebbles of perception;
    With poise and grace,
    accept what is,
    life's sharp embrace.
The pebbles of perception;
    Last to speak,
    seek better questions,
    to create, not critique.
The pebbles of perception;
    Choose their response,
    and cherish the choice,
    of needs, not wants.
The pebbles of perception;
    Seldom seek credit,
    self-aware, not self-absorbed,
    and never big-headed.
The pebbles of perception;
    With enthusiastic wonder,
    forge their character,
    without going under.
The pebbles of perception;
    Come what season,
    gently round out,
    the rocks of reason.
And in the end;
    Soft sand
    beneath the feet
    of children playing.

Appendix I – Still Curious?

Try to read widely and wisely. The cumulative effect over a long period is staggering. I started reading quite late in life, but hope to make up for it by eking out a few extra years at the back end.

With the ever-expanding reading choice our challenge is to avoid the rabbit holes. One suggestion is to look for the best books recommended by people whose judgement you respect.

The following highlights some of the people that I found to be excellent in their respective fields.

Thinking & Wisdom: Peter Bevelin, Edward de Bono, Benjamin Franklin, Daniel Gilbert, Daniel Kahneman, Jiddu Krishnamurti, Steven Pinker, Tania Singer, Amos Tversky.

Philosophy & Effective Living: James Allen, Stephen Covey, Viktor Frankl, Tamar Gendler's Open Yale philosophy lectures, Daniel Gilbert, Khalil Gibran, A.C. Grayling, Charles Handy, Tony Humphreys, Oriah Mountain Dreamer, Thomas Merton, Anthony de Mello, Shane Parrish's Farnam Street blog, M. Scott Peck, Graham Price, Eckhart Tolle.

Selling, Negotiation & Influence: Dan Ariely, Robert Cialdini, Herb Cohen, Stuart Diamond, Jeffrey Gitomer, Gavin Kennedy, Daniel Pink, Brian Tracy, William Ury.

Marriage: John Gottman.

Investing: Warren Buffett, Joel Greenblatt, Seth Klarman, Howard Marks, Michael Mauboussin, Charlie Munger, David Swensen.

If I had to narrow my recommendation down to a selection of just seven books to read, they would be as follows:

> *A New Earth* by Eckhart Tolle
> *Influence* by Robert Cialdini
> *Man's Emerging Mind* by N.J. Berrill
> *Poor Charlie's Almanack* by Charles T. Munger
> *Relationship, Relationship, Relationship*
>   by Tony Humphreys and Helen Ruddle
> *The Promise* by Graham W. Price
> *Thinking, Fast and Slow* by Daniel Kahneman

About the Author

Laurence Endersen spent his childhood in Mallow, a small town in the south of Ireland, and now lives with his family in Dublin.

Laurence is human, and despite his best intentions he doesn't always follow his own advice. Cobblers' kids and old shoes spring to mind.

Larry

Owen

Valerie

Eileen

Made in the USA
Middletown, DE
23 September 2015